INTEGRITY
SELLING®

INTEGRITY SELLING®

How to Succeed in Selling
in the Competitive Years Ahead

RON WILLINGHAM

DOUBLEDAY

NEW YORK LONDON TORONTO SYDNEY AUCKLAND

PUBLISHED BY DOUBLEDAY
A division of Bantam Doubleday Dell Publishing Group, Inc.
1540 Broadway, New York, New York 10036

DOUBLEDAY and the portrayal of an anchor with a dolphin
are trademarks of Doubleday, a division of Bantam Doubleday
Dell Publishing Group, Inc.

Library of Congress Cataloging-in-Publication Data
Willingham, Ron, 1932–
Integrity selling.
    1. Selling.   I. Title.
HF5438.25.W535 1987   658.8'5   86-23945
ISBN 0-385-23909-2

With appreciation . . .

Two people have played an important role in my life's work:

Dr. Maxwell Maltz

W. Clement Stone

What I learned from my association with them comes through many times in this book.

It's with deep gratitude and a strong sense of commitment that I share some of the knowledge that they've shared with me.

CONTENTS

Introduction

Not long ago an associate, Bill Brooks, and I trained a group of Chevrolet dealers to conduct one of my sales-training programs for their sales and customer contact people.

At the conclusion of the three-day seminar, Ken Wechselberger, director of Sales Training and Education for Chevrolet, stood and made this comment: "I'm totally convinced that this program is the vehicle we need to change the *culture* of our entire dealer network!"

Why did he say that? Because General Motors desires to upgrade the level of professionalism of their dealers. They well understand that to compete in the marketplace they'd better develop dealers and salespeople the public can trust and respect. They know that's as important as the quality of cars they produce.

I'm convinced that a lack of consumer trust plagues many salespeople today. It costs companies millions in unrealized sales and profits.

I begin most of the sales-training seminars I conduct by asking questions and getting two audience volunteers to write the responses on flip charts.

The first question is, "If we interviewed ten people on the streets of Anywhere, U.S.A., and asked them, 'What do you think of when you hear the word Salesman?,' what responses do you think we'd get?"

I almost always get the same answers. "Fast-talker." "High-pressure." "Con-man." "Used cars." "Manipulator." "Someone who's out to get me!"

You don't have to be too observant to see that these aren't very positive responses.

I introduce the next question by saying, "Let me ask you the same question again—only now I'll add a couple of new words. The question now is, 'What do you think of when I mention the term *Integrity Selling?*'"

Immediately I begin to get responses like "an honest process," "the way I like to be sold," "when someone sells the right thing to me," "selling me what I need or want," "what a physician does," or "forming trust relationships!"

After the responses are written on the flip chart, I ask the audience, "What characterizes the first set of responses?"

"They're all negative!" several immediately shout.

"And what characterizes the second set of responses?"

And just as immediately, several say, "They're all positive!"

"Yeah," I reply, "and *why* did they change?"

"Because you introduced the term Integrity Selling," they answer.

"That's right! It changed because I introduced a new term to the sentence. Because I introduced Integrity Selling!

"And, ladies and gentlemen, in my opinion, that's what has to happen for you to succeed in selling in the competitive years ahead. You must introduce integrity into your selling.

"You must learn and practice Integrity Selling!"

I believe that buyers are demanding more honesty and integrity from sellers. That's why I've written this book—to help you sell with integrity. To help you develop trust, respect, and professionalism.

The truth is that many buyers don't trust salespeople. They don't feel comfortable around them. They don't view them as respected professionals. So . . . they don't buy from them!

And why should they?

Because for as long as I can remember, salespeople and customers have been pitted against each other in an almost adversarial relationship—one where someone wins and someone loses!

Salespeople have been conditioned with bromides such as "sell 'em where they land," or "the sale begins when the customer says no!"

Or, how about this gem: "Close early and often!"

Traditionally, salespeople have been taught "101 tricky closes"—that selling is something you do *to* someone, not *for* and *with* someone!

The strategy has been for salespeople to outtalk, outmaneuver, outthink prospects. Even in television programs, salespeople have often been cast in roles that portray them as sleazy, manipulative, and without ethics.

No wonder people don't trust salespeople.

But a day of reckoning is upon us! Competition is stronger. No longer will sales gimmickry work in the marketplace. Buyers are getting smarter, more sophisticated, more demanding. They won't put up with all this old manipulative stuff anymore. They'll simply go somewhere else to buy.

And besides all that . . . our culture is changing.

Massive value shifts are occurring. Buyer tastes and levels of awareness are constantly being upgraded. And the whole world is competing for consumers' dollars.

All these rumblings are ushering in the need for changing the way the world sells.

Simply put, salespeople and businesses had better upgrade the way they sell, or they probably won't be around to sell a few years from now.

That's what this book is about: upgrading the way people sell.

I'll give you the techniques and the "how-to." But more important, I'll present to you a *system* of selling that's based on values and integrity. Then you'll learn how to apply this system to different styles of buyers.

You'll learn that different people buy things differently. Some make quick, impulsive decisions; others make slow, studied ones. Some make popular, emotional decisions; others make logical, fact-based ones. Some people are outgoing and friendly; others are cool and distant. Some are easygoing and accommodating; and still others are dominating and aggressive.

You'll learn how to identify these styles of buyers. You'll also learn how to match your own personal style with your prospect's. You'll discover that often mismatches have kept you from being successful in your selling.

I get many letters from people telling me what happened when they assimilated and applied my sales system. One recent letter read, "Thanks to you and your system, I recently closed what will be our company's largest single sale this year. I sold $345,000 in systems furniture to Popeye's Famous Fried Chicken."

He went on to say, "While the impact of that one sale is significant, the real impact is in the continued upturn in all sales across the board. Our other salespeople are able to recognize customers' needs more clearly. This leads to more calls per day and more dollars per month."

An insurance executive writes and says, "Your system has provided me with additional confidence because now I know exactly how to proceed in virtually all sales situations."

A computer store manager reports, "It is important to me that our training investment shows good returns. What we have experienced from your program is enhanced morale, increased activity, and most of all, a dramatic amount of additional closes. It has been an exciting change for my staff."

A real estate executive writes, "Your system makes the science of selling easy to understand for the novice as well as for the experienced salesperson. The system can stick with you during the heat of a sales presentation and keep you on track."

A life insurance regional sales manager writes, "I have already experienced exceptional results using your system. I fully expect sales in my region to increase a minimum of 50 percent this coming year as a result of using your simple, yet profound system."

A dentist writes, "Your approach to patients has a tremendous impact on our practice, with production increasing tremendously. The immediate change has been overwhelming! It has helped us tap the potential of existing work with our active patients. I purposely wanted to delay writing in that I wanted to assess our success after several months of using your system."

Well . . . I could go on and on sharing with you the actual benefits of real people who have assimilated and applied the system that you'll learn in this book.

I share these few examples to make the point that when you practice the ideas in this book you'll see results.

Throughout this book, I'll talk about the concept of Integrity Selling. I'll clearly state that I don't believe old-fashioned, traditional, manipulative sales strategies will bring success in the future.

I'll stress, over and over, that successful selling isn't a

question of tricky strategies and techniques; rather it's the result of proper values and ethics.

As I said, my belief is that we're experiencing massive cultural and value shifts in our country. Goods and services are plentiful. Buyers have lots of choices today—not only in products or services, but also in the integrity level of the people from whom they buy.

All around I see buyers becoming more selective in what they buy, and even more importantly, from *whom* they buy.

And I'm totally convinced that we'll see this wave of buyer motivation increase in the future—where they flock to trusted professionals and shun the ones who lack integrity. Plainly what I mean is that buyers will more and more look for high integrity in salespeople.

When you practice Integrity Selling, your customers will get the message quickly that you're a professional. They'll trust you more, refer friends to you more, and buy more from you.

A Statement of
Integrity Selling
Values and Ethics

1. Selling is an exchange of value.
2. Selling isn't something you do *to* someone, it's something you do *for* and *with* someone.
3. Understanding people's wants or needs must always precede any attempt to sell.
4. Develop trust and rapport before any selling activity begins.
5. Selling techniques give way to selling principles.
6. Integrity and high ethics are accepted as the basis for long-term selling success.
7. A salesperson's ethics and values contribute more to sales success than do techniques or strategies.
8. Selling pressure is never exerted by the salesperson. It's exerted only by prospects when they perceive they want or need the item being sold.
9. Negotiation is never manipulation. It's always a strategy to work out problems . . . when prospects *want* to work out the problems.
10. Closing isn't just a victory for the salesperson. It's a victory for both the salesperson and the customer.

INTEGRITY
SELLING®

1

How to Approach People

My objective in writing this book on professional selling is to help you increase your sales and communication skills.

It's to help you earn more money, increase your confidence with people, and demonstrate greater professionalism to your clients, customers, or prospects.

It's been my experience as a sales trainer that few salespeople have been taught that selling is a science.

Many books, tapes, and seminars have been produced that present selling as a bag of tricks. Tricky closes or cute manipulative tactics have been passed off as sales training.

My belief is that these tricky devices don't really work for most of us. In fact if we try to use them, most of us run into all kinds of inner conflicts.

A cognitive dissonance arises that becomes self-defeating.

All around me today I see big opportunities and big dollars just waiting for professional salespeople. People who practice selling with the skill, science, and integrity that a professional uses in any area.

This book will help you learn to practice selling as a science.

You'll learn a scientific six-step system of selling. Not only will you learn it, but you'll also be able to internalize it into your selling behavior—if you carefully follow all the directions I give you.

A big promise, you say?

Yes, it is. But I'll prove to you that I can deliver.

Just the other day a client of mine, Guyon Saunders, president of a company named Corporate Systems, told me that he'd made a sale, as a result of using my sales system, that has brought his company $300,000 per year in profit for five years.

He closed a sale that covered his company's expenses and overhead plus $300,000 per year profit for five years.

"I probably wouldn't have closed the deal if I hadn't used your system," he explained.

Then he explained that he was renegotiating the contract for another five years on top of the two that had just elapsed.

So . . . his company enjoyed a net income of over $2 million on just one sale, as a result of his professional selling.

I also have in my files a letter from Scott Gilmour, his vice president of sales, telling of a 41 percent increase in his company's other business over a previous year. He gave strong credit to our sales system for helping them achieve that increase.

I did a seminar for another client one year after training their salespeople to use my system.

After that first seminar their salespeople received a cassette album and a weekly follow-up.

At the second annual conference, the vice president of marketing told the group of over fifty salespeople that as a result of practicing my system, and in a down market, he could probably account for close to $10 million in sales they wouldn't have otherwise received.

I also teach my sales system to dentists. In one survey of over two hundred dental offices which used the system, they averaged reporting over $3,500 per week of increased revenue.

I could go on and on with statements from hundreds of individuals who've written and called about the sales increases they experienced after using my system.

The sales system I've designed is a logical process of selling. It makes the assumption that all good selling is filling needs, satisfying wants, or solving problems; that the only basis for making sales is solving problems, satisfying wants, or filling needs.

The Six-Step System of Selling

Here's the six-step system:

Approach . . . to gain rapport
Interview . . . to identify needs
Demonstrate . . . to explain features and benefits
Validate . . . to prove your claims
Negotiate . . . to work out problems
Close . . . to ask for a decision

So . . . you have these six steps. Approach, Interview, Demonstrate, Validate, Negotiate, and Close.

I call it the AID, Inc.® system. You can remember AID, Inc. if you remember that when you incorporate it into your selling, it's a sales aid that helps you be more successful.

Now you'll quickly see that AID stands for Approach, Interview, Demonstrate. But you may have problems fitting Validate, Negotiate, Close to the last Inc.

To make it fit we'll have to bend the way we spell "validate." We'll bend it and spell it val-I-date, and pronounce it val-eye-date.

The following graph represents the AID, Inc. system:

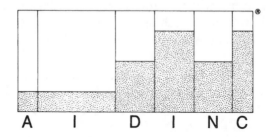

Notice the approximate percentage of the whole time that each step takes. Then notice the percentage of time in each step during which you talk (represented by the shaded-in area), as well as the percentage of time your customers talk (represented by the area above the shaded-in area).

You'll notice that in the first two steps you do only 20 percent of the talking, while you do 80 percent of the listening. This is quite different from what most salespeople do.

Here are three rules for using the system. Please read them, then stop a moment, look at the above graph, and think about them. They are:

1. Always find out where you are with your prospect and begin at that point.
2. Always complete one step before going to the next one.
3. Never jump to a step without completing the prior ones.

Once you understand this simple system, you'll have a road map to follow, as well as an instrument to give you feedback and reveal what went wrong when you didn't close.

You'll see that failure to close is always caused by failure to complete a step.

With this in mind, let's get into the first step of our sales system . . . the Approach step.

Your Approach Prepares People to Listen to You

An effective Approach prepares your clients, customers, or prospects to listen to you. It sets the stage. It breaks the preoccupation of both you and your customers. It also helps reduce their defensiveness. It helps you deal with the natural barriers that people put up when you come into contact with them.

You can't go wrong by assuming that people will always put up barriers when you approach them. They'll fold their arms, both physically and mentally.

I once called on a person whose desk was up on a riser. There were no chairs close to his desk, only a sofa several feet away that was very low to the floor. I kept waiting for him to pull a lever that would open a trapdoor and plunge me into an underground cavern.

Obviously he liked to intimidate salespeople.

One company I'm familiar with won't allow salespeople to call in the offices of purchasing executives. They're met in tiny cubicles that are all but lifeless.

You've probably seen your share of demonstrations of buyer defensiveness.

"Oh, I'm just looking!" is a common one in retailing.

So, let's talk about how you can break through shields and defenses; how you can deal with preoccupation; how you can gain rapport with people.

Here are four "action guides" for the Approach step—four ways to get people physically and psychologically unfolding their arms. Notice carefully what they are . . . and the actions they suggest:

1. Tune the world out and your prospects in.
2. Put them at ease and make them feel important.
3. Get them talking about themselves.
4. Hold eye contact and listen to how they feel.

Tune the World Out and Your Prospects In

Not long ago I was doing a seminar for dental professionals. During a break one doctor told me of a new patient
who'd just begun coming to his office.

After some initial probing, he found a very interesting
reason why the woman had left her previous doctor.

She told how on her last visit, the previous doctor had
been wearing something new: a headset with a cord dan-
gling from it. When he began his work, he plugged the cord
into his telephone and spent his time talking to his stock-
broker, rather than communicating with her.

She was steamed!

Kind of blatant . . . isn't it?

You say, "I would never do that."

But how often are salespeople guilty of figuratively talking to their stockbrokers? It's called preoccupation.

Here's a simple tip I learned many years ago that has
helped many people automatically break their preoccupa-
tions.

Whenever you approach someone, say to yourself, "At
this moment this is the most important person in the world
to me!"

Say that several times each day for three or four weeks
and you'll automatically begin to tune the world out and
your prospects in.

Put Them at Ease and Make Them Feel Important

The second action guide is "Put them at ease and make them feel important."

There's no greater human need than the need to feel important. When we begin filling that need, we meet open minds.

Get Them Talking About Themselves

I once called on a man who was the executive vice president of the largest financial organization of its kind in his state.

He was very busy. It was extremely difficult for me to get an appointment with him. I was given fifteen minutes. As I was ushered into his office suite, his secretary reminded me of the time limit in a very icy, businesslike way.

When I walked into his office and shook his hand, I noticed a stuffed pheasant on his credenza.

"Did you kill that pheasant?" I automatically asked.

"Yeah," he responded.

"Where did you get it?"

"In Nebraska," he said.

"That's a long way from here," I said. "As busy as you must be, how do you find time to go pheasant hunting that far away?"

I found real quickly that he didn't have as much time as he'd like to have, that his job was too demanding.

After talking about my question for a few minutes, he turned sideways to me, steepled his fingers, started rocking back and forth in his chair, and gazed out of his floor-to-ceiling plate-glass windows.

Then for most of two hours, he talked and I listened.

He started assessing his whole value system.

He mused on what success was all about; like, if working twelve to fifteen hours a day, weekends, and holidays was worth not getting to do things he liked to do—like pheasant hunting.

What I found out was that he'd just been waiting for someone to come along and ask him the right question . . . and then listen.

We developed a very strong rapport. I was able to put him at ease, make him feel important, and get him talking about himself. He didn't do it because I was pushy or dominant. He did it because he wanted to do it.

The fourth action guide for approaching people is "Hold eye contact and listen to how they feel."

Hold Eye Contact and Listen to How They Feel

The power of eye contact and emotional communication fascinates me. It has so much power in selling.

Let me share a story that makes this point.

Several years ago I was conducting one of my nine-week DynaGroup courses for a group of about twenty-five people. A young man stood and told a story that I've never forgotten.

He began by telling about being a soldier in Vietnam. One evening he and his buddies were pinned down in a bunker. His fellow soldiers were killed and he was hit three times—once each in his right shoulder, his right thigh, and his left side.

Lying on the ground, he thought that any moment he'd die. He visualized his heart pumping all the blood out of his left side . . . and then just quitting . . . and he'd be dead.

About that time the Vietcong soldiers came up and started going through the dead American soldiers' bodies—

taking their valuables—watches, rings, money, even knocking gold fillings out of their teeth.

One of the soldiers came up to him, reached down for his watch, and discovered he was still alive when the young man jerked his hand away. Immediately the enemy soldier pointed his gun between the young man's eyes. The young man just knew he was about to die.

He told how he looked up into the soldier's eyes, with as much feeling and emotion as he could muster, shook his head from side to side, and said, "No . . . no . . . please don't kill me!"

After a moment the enemy soldier could no longer handle it emotionally, broke eye contact, and pulled his gun away. Just then another Vietcong soldier yelled something. The young man assumed he asked if he was still alive, because the soldier yelled something back, which he assumed was "Yes." Then the other soldier yelled again. My friend assumed he yelled, "Kill him!" because once again the soldier pointed his gun at him and was about to pull the trigger.

Again, the young man looked deeply into his enemy's eyes, nodded his head from side to side, and said, "No . . . no . . . please don't kill me . . . please don't!"

After an incredibly painful pause, even though he couldn't understand the language, the Vietcong soldier once again backed down, broke eye contact, pulled his gun away, pointed it into the ground a few feet away, and pulled the trigger. He then yelled something to the other soldier, and walked away.

Did someone make a sale? Why? Did he overcome an objection? How? Did he communicate? How?

Interesting, isn't it?

It's also interesting to stop and really think about how much selling takes place in the first few minutes when we approach people.

Think for a moment . . . how often do you make assumptions about people immediately upon meeting them?

Pretty soon, you say? Don't we all? And upon what basis do we make these assumptions? Upon appearance? How people speak? Body language? Gestures? Emotions and feelings?

I live in a small townhouse complex in Amarillo, Texas. Eight other families live in it. One of our neighbors is a psychiatrist who loves plants and trees.

Often when he gets home, he'll put on some old jeans that are faded, an old shirt, and a floppy old golf hat. He then putters around the commons area talking to the trees.

Another one of our neighbors is a rather famous person, who, at the time, was trying to take over major oil companies. His name is T. Boone Pickens.

When he was trying to take over the Gulf Oil Company, his picture was in many newspapers, magazines, and financial journals. Cars were streaming in and out of our commons area wanting to see where he lives.

Dr. Pennal, the psychiatrist, was out in the entryway one afternoon, in his usual garb, having his conversation with an oak tree.

A car drove up, the driver rolled down his window and in a very demanding voice asked, "Hey you . . . tell me, which one of these places does Boone Pickens live in?"

The doctor casually eyed the man, ambled over to his car, scratched his head, and responded, "Don't ask me . . . I'm just the yardman here!"

Immediately the motorist said, "Uh, well, okay . . ." and rolled up his window and left.

Was a sale made? Upon what basis was it made? And how long did it take?

In Conclusion

Well . . . let me conclude this message by mentioning the Approach action guides again. They are:

1. Tune the world out and your prospects in.
2. Put them at ease and make them feel important.
3. Get them talking about themselves.
4. Hold eye contact and listen to how they feel.

Now, let me tell you how to get the most from this chapter.

1. Write these four action guides on an index card, and carry it with you all this next week.
2. Practice them every chance you get.
3. Reread this chapter two or three times this week. Read with a pen or pencil—underline, make notes, write in the margin.

Concentrate for one week on the Approach step. Practice, practice, practice. Each day analyze your practice.

This repetition will help you assimilate the guides and apply them to your selling habits.

Then go to chapter 2 the second week. When you follow these suggestions you'll harness the power of concentrated effort and repetitive learning.

This method of learning will influence your selling skills. It will program your mind to do these actions instinctively and automatically. Your natural sales skills will increase.

I'll assure you that as you practice the AID, Inc. system, some great things will happen to you.

INTEGRITY SELLING
SUCCESS PRINCIPLE

People are more apt to listen to you when they feel good about you—when they feel they can trust you!

2

How to Approach
Different Styles of Buyers

Several years ago I called on the president of a large bank. I was trying to sell him a training course for his employees. It was a course that we had had in other banks with very positive response.

I asked for thirty minutes of his time, and after about five minutes I could tell that I wasn't connecting with him at all.

He was giving me all kinds of those "positive" signals that salespeople love to get—looking at his watch and waving to bank customers as they passed by. At one point he interrupted me, jumped up, and told a man to have a seat, that he'd be ready to go to lunch in a couple minutes—just as soon as he was finished with me.

That certainly was a neat feeling!

I quickly told him how my training course would help his

employees have more confidence, like themselves more, be nicer to customers, and have better morale.

He was yawning and fidgeting.

Then, after about eight minutes, he interrupted me and said in a very plain, straightforward, difficult-to-misunderstand manner, "Look . . . we're not interested in anything like this. If our employees want to be better people, let 'em go to church! We're running a bank!"

With this he got up, ushered me out of his office, and went to lunch with his friend.

"Don't you usually get more *facts* before you make a decision?" I shot at him as he left me. I was fuming inside.

My whole afternoon was spent steaming.

The next day he called me and, with no emotion whatever, apologized and invited me to lunch. I made some excuse about being busy. The truth was that the last thing I wanted to do was go to lunch with him.

What I know now, but didn't know then, is that I completely missed communicating with him because I was communicating out of an emotional, feeling base, while he was buying out of a purely logical, rational base.

I was telling him how wonderful everyone would feel if they took my course, but that didn't communicate at all. He didn't hear a word I said.

Of course, at the time, I blamed *him* for my inability to communicate.

Now, after several years of learning about the different behavioral styles of people, I blame myself when I don't communicate with people.

Different People Exhibit Different Styles of Buying

When it first dawned on me several years ago that people showed different behavioral styles when buying, I began to try to identify the differences.

Two basic characteristics appeared. First, people were motivated by a need for recognition or a need for security.

Second, people were either task-oriented or results-oriented.

So for several years I taught that people buy because of what the product or service will do for them, or for how it'll make them look to others.

But then other factors began to come into focus.

After many years of attempting to learn, I've developed the following classification of buyer styles:

You'll notice that I've categorized the four buyer styles as Talkers, Doers, Plodders, and Controllers.

You'll also notice that the scale is shaped much like a clock dial—indicating the different levels or degrees that people fit into.

Now, few people fit totally into one style—most people are combinations of styles. But most people have predominant leanings toward one style.

Let me take a few moments and discuss each of the styles. Then we'll talk about how you approach each style —how you apply AID, Inc. to the buyer styles. As far as I know, this is the first time this kind of analysis has been done.

Talkers Are Social Types

Talkers love people. They love to visit and socialize. They like block parties, family reunions, bowling leagues. They're easy to gain rapport with—easy to approach. After ten minutes you'll think you've been friends for life.

Talkers like to tell jokes. When you hear the preface, "Hey, have you heard the one about . . . ," you'll know you're probably communicating with a Talker.

Talkers enjoy chitchat. They're friendly and affable. They often have a cluttered environment. Their automobile interiors usually need cleaning. They like pictures and things that bring them recognition. They're often more daring with their dress and jewelry.

A few years ago our firm was conducting three-day career development seminars for Department of Labor–related agencies. I called on a man in a seven- or eight-state regional office. I was told that he was a decision-maker.

The moment I walked into his office it was like we were old buddies. He got up, came around his desk, shook my hand with his right hand, and covered both our hands with his left one.

He then walked me over to where two guest chairs were, seated me, and sat down beside me.

He was so glad to see me . . . it appeared.

I got all excited, thinking that I had an easy sale here. Everything was extremely positive.

After a few minutes, he began looking at his watch. He did this several times. I couldn't figure it out because he was giving no other signs of wanting me to leave.

Then about the fifth time he looked at his watch, he bolted out of his chair, ran over to the window ledge, picked up a long telescope, pulled it open, and began peering out of his fourth-story window.

Immediately he began to make all kinds of crazy sounds, while motioning frantically for me to come over to the window.

I thought there'd been an assassination or a palace revolt or some other history-making event. But when I got to the window I saw that he was watching several females leaving his building for lunch.

He named each one's anatomy, along with all sorts of appropriate sounds and motions.

Immediately I knew it was a daily game he played. And I also knew that I wasn't going to make a sale because he probably didn't have the authority to buy.

Sure enough, he didn't. As it turned out he was a front man for the real decision-maker—who controlled everything, holed up in a corner office.

But it was a very interesting lesson.

He had a terrific time during my visit. We got along great, especially when I asked him at what point he went from being a dirty *young* man to a dirty *old* man. That question made his day.

It's comforting to know that our tax dollars are spent on such efficient public servants!

Doers Are Achievers, Drivers

The second style of buyers is Doers. Their objective is to get things done.

Doers are often impatient, type A behavior people. There's never enough time. They're competitive and energetic. They attack things that get in their way. They talk about achievement, bottom-line results. There's often a free-floating hostility against anyone or anything that tries to slow them down.

A Doer's motto is "I don't want a forty-hour week, I want a forty-hour day!"

They like you to get to the point. They're impulsive and will make decisions based on gut feelings. They're very decisive, and will make quick decisions once they *think* they have a grasp of the necessary facts and information.

Doers are often surrounded by trophies, awards, plaques. They exhibit and talk about goals and rewards for achievement. Often you'll see their pictures with other well-known high-achievers.

They're restless and have nervous mannerisms.

Plodders Are Stable, Even-Tempered People

Plodders are content with routine, redundant jobs. They're usually never very high or very low. They're not pushed for time and are unhurried.

They like to do their jobs well, and are usually honest and dependable. They're the first ones in in the mornings and the last ones to leave in the evenings.

Plodders aren't risk-takers. They *don't* make quick decisions. They're motivated by security. They focus on doing good jobs, rather than getting high results. They're detail-minded—for the sake of doing the details well.

Plodders like to hang on to tried-and-true things, methods, and techniques.

I have a friend who's an accountant. Everything about him is neat and precise. Everything in his office has been neat and precise for forty years, too.

He still uses a Comptometer—a nonelectric calculator popular in the 1940s and early 1950s.

Most of you probably don't know what a Comptometer is. It has dozens of keys that can be punched with different finger positions in order to add, multiply, or divide.

His motto is "If it still works, don't throw it away or replace it . . . keep using it."

Controllers Are Logical, Rational People

Controllers are highly organized and show high attention to detail. Their decisions revolve around facts and figures. They don't make emotional decisions.

A controller's motto is "A place for everything and everything in its place!" They're surrounded by orderliness.

They talk about methods, conditions, and functions. They file information neatly and know how to retrieve it quickly when needed. They reveal a high degree of organization. Their desks may be loaded with work to be done, but it's all stacked in neat piles.

Controllers make good use of their time. They show high attention to details for the sake of efficient management. They also exhibit low emotional responsiveness.

Throughout this book you'll learn more about the different buyer styles. You'll also learn how to match your style with the different buyers', and how to use the AID, Inc. system to do it.

How to Approach Each Style

Here are some suggestions about how to approach each of the four styles I mentioned. These are clues to building rapport with them.

It's important to remember that we approach different people in different ways. We also use different amounts of time when we approach different people.

Look at your AID, Inc. graph and you'll see the approximate percentage of time each step takes. You'll notice that the Approach step takes up a small amount of the total selling time.

You'll also notice again that in the Approach step you do 20 percent of the talking and 80 percent of the listening.

This is a general statement, as you may find it more difficult to get Controllers and Plodders to do 80 percent of the talking. Talkers and Doers will easily do 80 percent of the talking because Talkers love to talk, and Doers love to dominate.

The secret is knowing the right kind of questions to ask each style.

You see . . . each style of buyer wants to communicate differently.

For instance, Talkers like to answer these kinds of approach questions:

- "How have you been doing?"
- "Where are you going on vacation?"
- "Where will you spend the holidays?"
- "What do you do for recreation or hobbies?"
- "Tell me about your children (or family members)."
- "What do you enjoy most about the people you know?"

You'll find that Talkers are easy to gain rapport with. Since they like people, as well as to talk, they'll often do 95 percent of the talking . . . or more!

Doers usually don't have time for chitchat. So don't ask them unimportant, how's-the-weather questions.

You can often misread Doers and not spend enough time in approaching them, though. While it's true that they don't have time for idle conversation, I've found that when I ask them the right questions they'll often take plenty of time to talk to me.

The secret lies in knowing the right kind of questions to ask, and knowing when they want to move on.

Here are some sample questions that I've asked Doers. Notice the type of questions they are:

- "How do you manage to get so much done?"
- "What are some secrets you've learned about managing your time?"
- "What are some things that have helped you get where you are today?"
- "What does it take to be successful in your position?"
- "How are you able to juggle so many different responsibilities?"
- "What advice would you give to someone who wants to achieve your level of success?"

My experience is when I ask these kinds of questions, it's easy to get Doers doing lots of talking. I've made many sales this way. I've also developed strong, ongoing selling relationships this way.

Here are some Approach questions that you can ask Plodders. Notice the characteristics of these questions:

- "How did you learn to do your work?"
- "What are some of the important functions of your job?"
- "What activities do you most enjoy doing?"
- "Why is keeping up with details so important?"
- "How do you keep everything looking so nice?"
- "How do you stay so calm and in control of yourself?"

Remember that Plodders want to talk about security and removing risks. They want to tell you why it's better to be "safe than sorry."

Again, it makes no difference whether you're making one sale to a person or if you call on the same people over and over. These ideas will work for you.

Here are some types of Approach questions to ask Controllers. Remember, Controllers are logical, no-nonsense buyers.

- "What's your secret for being so well organized?"
- "How do you keep up with so many facts and so much information?"
- "How are you able to lay your hands on information so quickly?"
- "What are the most important elements that keep your organization functioning?"
- "How are you able to use your time so well?"
- "What are some problem-solving techniques that work for you?"

Analyze these questions for a moment and you'll see that they tend to focus on logic and facts. Controllers like to talk about efficiency and good organization.

These suggestions may help you to approach different people successfully. It's not so important to remember the questions as to understand the principles behind them—to understand the type of questions to ask the different styles.

Don't expect to master these ideas instantly. They take time.

Also, I want to encourage you to read this chapter over and over. Begin to observe the differences in people you meet. Stop, look, and listen—*really* listen to people. You'll be amazed how much better you can communicate with people as you learn more about buyer styles.

Don't Try to Analyze Style While in Front of Someone

Maybe the most important thing I have to say in this message is that when you get in front of a prospect, customer, or client, *don't* try to analyze their style. Don't analyze when in front of someone.

If you analyze while trying to sell people, you'll probably

become preoccupied. This can interfere with your listening to what they're really trying to tell you.

Does this advice sound confusing? Then keep reading.

I've found that it's best to do my homework *before* contacting people. I try to learn as much as I can about them and I try to determine their styles. Then I structure my approach question, slanted toward their particular style.

When I'm in front of them I don't think about behavior styles, I just plug in and listen. I absorb and match their pace, tone, and attitude.

Then, *after* I call on them, I analyze the communication and what I saw in their environment. I role-play my encounter. I analyze what I did and how I could have better related to the person's style.

But while I'm in front of someone, I don't try to analyze them. I just tune into them. I try to feel how they feel, have empathy with them. I adjust to their emotional drumbeat.

I've learned that all the things I've mentioned in this chapter should be preprogrammed and then done subconsciously—automatically. Again, the preoccupation that you'll have trying to analyze someone's style when you're in front of them can be self-defeating.

These ideas can help you better understand the whole process of approaching different types of people in different ways.

In Conclusion

Here are some suggestions for getting the most benefits from this chapter.

1. Write down on an index card the four buyer styles. Under each style, write down two or three words that best characterize that style.

2. Carefully watch and observe clues people give you that reveal their predominant style.
3. Begin communicating to the style you identify, rather than through your own style.

Each day this week, begin to structure and plan your Approach so that it fits the person with whom you're communicating.

Remember to consciously practice the Approach action guides each time you contact people—whether it's the first time or the fifteenth.

Follow these ideas and you'll know more than most of your competitors will ever know about approaching people!

And your customers will notice a difference in you!

INTEGRITY SELLING
SUCCESS PRINCIPLE

People are more apt to buy from you when they perceive you view the world as they view the world!

3

How to Interview and Find Out People's Needs

In the Interview step you discover a person's wants or needs.

My belief is that people only buy products or ideas for their own end-result benefits.

You don't *sell* products or services to people; they buy them when they perceive they'll fill their needs, satisfy their wants, or solve their problems.

Experience tells me that most salespeople don't know what I've just told you.

For a moment let's take a look at traditional selling methods.

Years ago I was taught an old selling formula—AIDA. It stood for attention, interest, desire, action.

The theory was that a salesperson should go in and do something to get the prospect's attention. It might be by making an arresting statement, by a provocative question, or by doing a tricky demonstration.

Then, once attention had been gained, interest was to be aroused. This was usually done by giving a sales demonstration—by selling features, advantages, and benefits. By exciting the prospects with such things as "power phrases" and "word pictures."

Once interest had been aroused, desire was to be cultivated. Again, information was given to create desire—to "make 'em want it."

Then, after desire had been cultivated, the next step was to get action—to close.

This brought into being 60 billion different tricky closes. The objective seemed to be that if you outsmart people and outmaneuver them verbally, they'll have to say yes and buy.

Many books have been written about gimmicky closing techniques. They fill the shelves of bookstores. And, they sell . . . because, I suppose, many people are looking for tricks and magic that will open up new vistas of wealth and sales success.

I call this old-fashioned method "stimulus/response selling." It's characterized by these ingredients:

1. The salesperson does most of the talking.
2. The salesperson makes a "pitch" or presentation, attempting to sell whatever they're selling, rather than identifying the prospect's wants or needs, and attempting to fill them.
3. The salesperson assumes the selling posture that he or she is doing something *to* the prospect —not *for* them.

The selling process of the past has focused on this third ingredient: selling goods or services *to* people, not filling their needs.

Today . . . Old-Fashioned Sales Techniques Don't Work So Well

But today, things are changing. People are more educated and sophisticated. There's more competition—both domestic and foreign.

Today's sales professionals, the folks who earn big incomes selling, are into a different process.

Today, professional selling is based on need-fulfillment or need-satisfaction. The focus has totally changed.

Today's pros go out and look for problems to be solved, wants to be satisfied, needs to be filled.

Their manner of selling has a totally different slant.

What is it? Hang on—because that's what this whole book is about . . . especially this chapter.

Selling Isn't Selling, It's Need-Fulfillment

Burn this into your brain—*selling isn't selling, it's need-fulfillment.*

Recently I was in San Francisco doing a seminar and had a couple of hours to kill before catching a cab to the airport. So I went out walking around and walked into a Brooks Brothers store.

Walking through the men's suits section, a salesperson approached me with this very typical approach, "A forty-two long, heh?"

"Well . . . yeah," I responded.

"Then let me show you what we have in your size," he said, pointing to the beginning and ending of forty-two long suits.

Then he told me how long his firm had been in business

and that they'd pioneered the natural-shoulder, traditional look in clothing many years ago.

I knew that already.

I saw a grey, pinstriped suit, pointed it out, and looked at it.

"That would look good on you," he assured me. "It'll wear like iron. . . ."

Now I don't know about you, but I don't particularly want something that "wears like iron." I could get steel armor if that's what I wanted.

Then the salesman did what most salespeople do—he tried to sell me the suit I seemed to like.

Now, stop and think about this for a moment.

When you think, you'll see that this stimulus/response method of selling is how most salespeople attempt to sell things.

But if you go into a men's clothing store that I've held sales meetings for, you'll see something quite different.

You'll be approached with a friendly "Thank you for coming into our store . . . we're happy to have you."

Then the salespeople would ask a couple of simple, nonthreatening Approach questions, like "Have you been in our store before?" "How long has it been since you've been in?" "Do you live in the city?"

Then they'll put you at ease and take the pressure *off* you by asking "Are you looking for something special . . . or would you just like to look around?"

When you show interest in a suit, for instance, the salespeople wouldn't try to sell you whatever you'd be willing to buy, they'd do an interview.

Now read carefully!

Their interview is prefaced with this statement: *"In order for me to help you get the best value, may I ask you a few questions?"*

After getting permission, they begin to ask some questions. As they ask and get responses, they write down important information on a leather-covered note pad.

What kind of questions do they ask? Here are some samples. Notice how they're both open-ended and indirect:

> "What kind of work or profession are you in?"
> "What kind of image do you want to portray?"
> "Where will you be wearing this suit?"
> "What color or style are you considering?"
> "What other colors do you now have?"
> "How long will you plan to keep it?"
> "Describe to me the suits that you've enjoyed the most."

These and other questions are learned by the salespeople. The customers talk a lot, feeling no pressure. The salesperson then learns about the needs and wants of the customer, and is in a position to show what will best satisfy their wants or needs.

The Purpose of Interview Questions

Here's the whole purpose of the interview process:

1. To get the customers doing 80 percent of the talking and the salesperson doing 20 percent.
2. To help the salesperson understand the customer's wants or needs.
3. To help the customers discover, verbalize, and clarify their own wants or needs.
4. To let the customers know, with actions, that the salesperson isn't just trying to sell them *anything*, but wants to help them select the *best value*.

See the difference? Which salesperson would you feel more comfortable with? Which do you feel is more professional?

I'm constantly amazed at how little most salespeople know about selling! Most think that selling is telling someone about the product or service they sell. So they dominate the talking and explain features.

I was in Las Vegas recently conducting a seminar. The evening before I walked over to a shopping center and went into Neiman-Marcus to look through the men's clothing section. I saw an Oxxford suit that I liked. The salesman talked endlessly about the fine quality of it. He was a very nice man. He had a lot of pride in his products. He had high product-knowledge.

But not once did he ask me what I did, what else I wore, how I would wear it, or anything like that. He obviously didn't think about interviewing me to get information.

I bought it . . . but he didn't sell me!

Interview Action Guides

Now that I've shared these examples with you, let me mention the four action guides for the Interview step. These are four things to do in order to interview and discover people's wants or needs successfully.

1. Ask open-ended, indirect questions that draw out wants or needs.
2. Listen to and paraphrase all points—write them down.
3. Identify dominant wants or needs—get the prospect's agreement.
4. Assure prospects that you want to help them select the right product or service.

Before I go on, let me mention that when I say "prospect" I'm referring to whatever you call the people you sell your services or products to—whether you call them clients, customers, patients, or other names.

The heart of the Interview step is asking what I call need-development questions. Need-development questions are open-ended, indirect questions that draw out wants or needs.

This isn't an easy step to take because it demands some reprogramming. If you're used to immediately selling, telling, or demonstrating, this type of selling will seem different and probably a bit uncomfortable at first.

So hang in with me and let me take you through the step-by-step process of designing your own need-development questions.

Identify the Wants or Needs Your Customers Have

The first step sounds simple—but it isn't.

To help you identify your customer's wants or needs, let me share this concept with you:

> People don't buy your product or service because you want them to or because of what it is. They buy it because of what it'll *do* for them . . . or because of how it'll make them *look* to others!

Understanding this is the basis for understanding need-fulfillment selling.

Here's what I mean:

- People don't want their teeth straightened just to have their teeth straightened. They want it because it'll help them *look* better and have a better smile.
- People don't buy clothing because of the fiber content. They buy clothing because the fabric will wear well and hold its shape and they'll *look* good.
- People don't buy automobiles because of the technical features of the engine. They buy because they

like the style, or it gets good mileage, or it's better than their neighbor's.

- Companies don't buy computers because of the advanced circuitry. They buy them to promote more efficiency, give better and faster information, or save on work hours.

As you think of these ideas, take a few moments and ask yourself these questions:

"What is the end-result benefit that I give customers?"

"What problems do my products or services solve for them?"

"Why would they want to buy what I'm selling?"

"How can I help people enjoy higher recognition and self-esteem?"

"What risks will my product or service help neutralize?"

"How can I help customers look better to others?"

"How will I create more peace of mind for people?"

"How can I help people be healthier and more attractive?"

"How will I help customers enjoy greater profits or pleasure?"

Answering these questions can help you understand the *real* needs you fill. They can help you understand exactly what business you're in.

Getting Information Helps You Understand People's Wants or Needs

Then after you identify your customer's needs or wants, the next step is to think about the specific types of information you need to get—so you can specifically *understand* your customer's wants or needs.

Here are some different kinds of information you may need to get:

- What they've been using
- What they're looking for that they haven't found
- What quantity they purchase
- What budget or price range
- What their degree of interest is
- What problems they want to solve
- Who else will be involved in the purchase decision
- How open they are to new ideas.

As you'll see, getting this type of information helps you in several ways:

- It helps your customers discover and verbalize their own needs or wants.
- It gets them talking and you listening.
- It helps you qualify them.
- It helps *you* understand *their* wants or needs.
- It causes objections to surface.

Asking Need-Development Questions

To get this information you ask need-development questions. The questions are easy to design once you identify the information you want to get. You simply phrase a question for each kind of information you need.

Let me give you some examples of need-development questions.

Let's suppose I'm selling automobiles and you come into my showroom. Instead of showing you all the cars we have and then trying to sell you the one you seem to like the best, I'd approach and interview you.

After a quick approach I'd ask, "In order for me to help you select the best automobile for your needs, may I ask you a few questions?" Here are some sample need-development questions I might ask:

> "What kind of car have you been driving?"
> "How long have you had it?"
> "What have you enjoyed most about it?"
> "What difference, if any, are you looking for in a new one?"
> "How will you use the car—for work, pleasure, or family?"
> "How long do you plan to keep it?"
> "Who else besides you will be driving it?"
> "What will you be trading in on it?"

There are other important qualifying questions that could be asked, but you get the idea of this strategy.

Think for a moment and you'll see how much information can be learned by asking these questions.

Also, let me repeat that asking questions, listening, and writing them down puts your customers in the position of selling *themselves*.

This is the strongest selling strategy I know anything about.

In this strategy we *listen* people into buying, rather than *talk* them into buying!

It would be very profitable to stop and mull over the statement I've just made. *We* listen *people into buying, rather than* talk *them into buying.* This has helped thousands of salespeople's sales skyrocket!

It's only by listening that we can really understand people's wants or needs.

But it works on an even deeper level. There's a bonding that takes place when we listen. This emotional connection causes people to *want* to buy from us.

Again, take a few moments and think about the preceding statement.

This Strategy Puts You in an Integrity Selling Role

This whole process of need-fulfillment selling puts you into a consultative role. Prospects and customers get the feeling that you're there not to sell them anything they'll buy, but to help them select and enjoy the best *value.*

This strategy creates trust and heightens rapport—which are the bases for all successful sales careers.

Let me wrap up this chapter by repeating the action guides for the Interview step. They are:

1. Ask open-ended, indirect questions that draw out wants or needs.
2. Listen to and paraphrase all points—write them down.
3. Identify dominant wants or needs—get the prospect's agreement.
4. Assure prospects that you want to help them select the right product or service.

In Conclusion

Let me share with you how to gain the most benefits from this session:

1. Read this chapter several times this week.
2. Write down the Action Guides on an index card and carry it with you as a reminder to practice them.
3. Write out a list of each of your customer's needs and the information you need to get from them so you understand their needs.
4. Design eight or ten specific need-development questions, memorize them, and begin asking them immediately.

As you ask need-development questions, expect to be a bit uncomfortable at first. Any new habit creates some discomfort. After three or four weeks, you'll get more comfortable asking them . . . instead of immediately selling, telling, or demonstrating.

Then, as you ask your need-development questions, analyze your results. Polish your questions constantly so they're smooth and indirect, and not leading or manipulative.

As you do these actions, your selling will take on a new professionalism. Your customers will trust you more, feel less pressure from you, and buy more from you.

You'll discover a whole new level of opportunities for your sales career.

INTEGRITY SELLING
SUCCESS PRINCIPLE

People are more apt to buy when *they're* talking than when *you're* talking!

4

How to Interview
Different Styles of Buyers

Professional salespeople have the knack of relating to different styles of buyers.

Some do it naturally and almost instinctively. Others learn how to do it.

Some years ago our firm was giving job-skills seminars to unemployed people for federally funded agencies around the country.

Several of the agencies with whom we worked referred us to a person whose name was Billy Don Everett. He headed an area of several counties in central Texas.

One of my staff people called and, after some difficulty, made an appointment for me to go call on Billy Don.

His office was about five hundred miles from where I lived, so it took a whole day to fly down, rent a car, and call on him.

My appointment was for three-thirty one afternoon. I believe in always showing up early, so I arrived about two forty-five.

He wasn't in then. When I asked what time he'd be in, a receptionist said, "Oh, you never can tell about Billy Don . . . you never know for sure when he's going to show up."

"I have a three-thirty appointment with him," I reminded her, to which she smiled at me as if to say "and how about some swamp land in Florida?"

Well, three-thirty came, and no Billy Don. Three forty-five, then four o'clock. Then about four-fifteen he sauntered in.

He looked at me and asked, "Are you still here?"

"Well, uh, yeah," I replied, rather defensively.

"Well, you're wasting your time," he shot back.

"I am?"

"Yeah, I told that boy that called me that I wasn't interested in your training. You're just wasting your time!"

Groping for some response I said, "What did he say when you told him that?"

"Aw, he asked me why didn't I make a decision *after* I talked to you, instead of before."

Then he went on, "Oh well, as long as you're here, you might as well tell me what you've got. How much is it?"

Ducking his question, I explained that I had videotaped highlights of a seminar we'd done for another agency.

"Well, turn it on," he demanded with about as much excitement as a person being strapped into an electric chair.

So against my better judgment, as well as my sales system, I flipped on the videotape. It was about twenty minutes long.

About halfway through it, he got up without saying a word, stretched, and left the room. He just left! Leaving me with two of his staff people.

"Where's Billy Don going?" I asked.

"Who knows?" one responded. "You never know about Billy Don!" That had a familiar ring.

When the videotape finished, I nervously made small talk with the two people. In a few minutes Billy Don wandered back in.

"You still here?" he asked.

By this time, I was ready to kill him. He seemed to sense this, and sensing it gave him all kinds of pleasure.

He walked over, turned an armless chair around backward, sat down in it, put his forearms on the back, grinned at me and said, "Okay, sell me!"

Immediately thoughts started going through my head. Like "If I kill him right here, would that be first-degree murder . . . or just manslaughter? Would I just get life . . . or death by hanging?"

For a couple of seconds I just looked at him, trying to figure out what to do.

"Why not gamble?" I thought. "What have you got to lose?"

So I pulled my chair up real close to him, looked squarely into his right eyeball, and said, "Billy Don, Willie Taylor [a friend of his] told me that you run the *worst* office in the whole state!"

Saying that I then shut up and just looked at him.

In a moment, he just died laughing! He roared!

"Did he really say that?" he asked.

"No, he didn't," I said. "He said that you run a very efficient office. But he also told me that you'd try to con me and give me a line of bull ten feet deep!"

He grinned as if I'd paid him the highest compliment possible. He relaxed. We visited. I found out that his high-school football coach was a friend of mine.

I also discovered that he wanted to be confronted. I'd ask a question or make a statement and, every time, he'd take exception to it.

It was only when I began responding, "Oh, Billy Don, you

don't know what you're talking about!" that he really liked me.

I got all the information I needed after that. He gladly and willingly told me everything I needed to know. Before I left we agreed on the terms of the training I'd do for him, where we'd do it, and when.

At the end of the interview, I told him how I appreciated his business, that we'd do a very good job for him, and that if he needed more references I'd be happy to give them to him.

As I was leaving, he got real serious and paid me the highest compliment any genuine Texas redneck could pay. He said, "I'll tell you one thing, I'd sure as hell hate to get into a poker game with you!"

I smiled and said, "Billy Don, you'd win everything!"

He liked that. And we became good friends.

Let me ask you, what need did I fill for him that caused him to buy? How would you have classified Billy Don? A Talker, a Doer, a Controller, or a Plodder? Or what combination?

I'll let you figure that one out for yourself.

As near as I could tell, his dominant buying motive was that he liked me and that he wanted more recognition from his peers. He didn't want to be the only director in the state who hadn't used our training.

But he also wanted his teenaged son to be in the training so he'd be a better athlete.

I know all this because I asked indirect questions and listened. I also knew that he'd be motivated to buy, or not to buy, on impulse.

How did I know that? Because everything about him from his time management to his listening span was impulsive. He moved when, and if, he wanted to.

Asking the Right Questions

One of the biggest sales I ever made, from the standpoint of actual and potential income, was made to the Shaklee Corporation. I sold them a proposal that I write a weight-management program for them. The program is called "Slim Up & Live" and large numbers of people now go through it.

When I first approached their then vice president of sales, he let me know very quickly that I had thirty minutes, that he had no interest in my doing any training work for them, that every trainer in the business had been trying to sell them stuff, and that the only reason he was seeing me was that a mutual friend had asked him to do so.

Everything about him was busy, chaotic. He had incredible time demands.

I thanked him for being honest with me and went right into my interview.

"How does your number of active sales leaders compare with two years ago?" I asked.

He sputtered and admitted that they were down some.

"Yes, I understand they are," I responded.

"And what's happening to this product line [I mentioned a specific one] since your projections a year ago?"

Again he sputtered and said, "Okay, what do you want?"

I had some other need-development questions written down. Like "What are some economic factors that have affected your business?" "What kind of training do you now provide for your field people?"

My first thirty-minute appointment lasted about two hours. An excellent rapport was developed. I understood some of his needs—from his viewpoint. And the door was open for decisions that ultimately led to an agreement that is selling lots of products for them.

It would have been inappropriate to have wasted his time

with chitchat or small talk. He wanted to get right to the subject at hand. But when I asked the right questions, he responded with interest . . . and had plenty of time to talk, despite his chaotic schedule.

Different Types of Questions for Different Types of Buyers

Let me outline several types of Interview questions you can ask different styles of buyers.

For Talkers, here are some interview questions. Carefully notice the types of questions:

- Ask *who* will be involved in using the product or service.
- Ask what other people like, or don't like, about what they've been using.
- Ask how employee morale will be influenced.
- Ask who else will be involved in the final decision.
- Ask how they *feel* about your offering.

A Talker may purchase a computer because it makes another employee happy, or because it causes someone to like him or her better.

Talkers may buy from you because they like you, or because you have lunch with them or drink coffee with them.

Need for recognition is a strong influence with them— also the need to please others . . . even you, the seller.

Here are some types of questions to ask Doers in your interview. Notice the common thread that runs through them:

- Ask what they want to *accomplish*.
- Ask what they want to happen that isn't now happening.
- Ask what you can do to save their time.

- Ask about the importance of their getting more done.
- Ask what problems they have that *you* can help them solve.

Remember that Doers don't demand a lot of details. Since their main concern is causing results, remember to talk in terms of results. Also, remember to take care of as many details for them as you can.

Doers have a high need for recognition, but not the same kind of recognition as Talkers. Talkers want you to like them because they want to be liked. Doers want you to respect them because of their achievements. Often they don't really care whether you like them or not.

Then, here are some types of questions to ask Controllers. Remember that Controllers are interested in organization, good management, efficiency, and overall smooth functioning.

- Ask what *return on investment* they're looking for.
- Ask what would help their organization run more efficiently.
- Ask questions that call for facts and specific answers.
- Ask for their opinions.
- Ask how they *manage* functions, jobs or themselves so efficiently.

Don't expect Controllers to spend a lot of time visiting. They want to move on. Since they're fact or logic oriented, you must be fact and logic oriented when you ask questions and when you give them responses. Your emotional responsiveness must match theirs—which is often cool and controlled.

Plodders, since they're stable, dependable people, want to talk about stable, dependable things. They feel comfortable when *you're* stable and dependable—when they feel they can trust you.

You don't need to hurry your interview with Plodders. If they think seeing you is important, they'll take plenty of time.

Here are some categories of questions you should ask Plodders. Notice the nature of these questions:

- Ask what would *help* them do their jobs better.
- Ask them what risks you can help them avoid.
- Ask them what details they want explained.
- Ask them what's worked well for them in the past.
- Ask them to help *you* out.

Take a moment and reread these types of Interview questions that you can ask different styles of buyers. Notice the differences. Notice the principles of communication involved.

This will help you become aware of the different types of people and the different ways they want you to communicate with them. Really listen and notice the clues that reveal people's styles.

As you Interview to find out people's needs, listen to their tone of voice. Listen to their emotional responsiveness. Listen to their energy level. Listen to their pacing. Listen to their response time—how long they take to think and answer.

Doing these activities will help you become more and more observant of people's needs: their need for your product or service. Their need for recognition. Their need to look good. Their need to remove risks. Their need for you to listen to them. Their need to trust you.

As You Listen and Observe You'll Discover Many Types of Needs

As you become more and more observant of people, you'll also discover that the real needs that cause people to buy aren't always the obvious ones.

In 1954, just out of college, I got a job as an outside salesman for an office-equipment firm. One of my accounts was a dairy, and the person I called on was the office manager.

He was a surly old man who apparently "had a mad on" for the whole world. Every time I called on him he'd chew me up and spit me out. I always dreaded having to see him.

One day I was in his office and he interrupted me and said, "You must be the worst salesman I've ever seen!"

Now, *that* was a happy experience!

What I wanted to say was "No . . . I couldn't be the worst *salesman* in the world . . . that would be too much of a coincidence!"

But I didn't! Instead I asked, "Well, why don't you tell me how I can be a better one?"

He rallied to that challenge. For about an hour, he gave me advice on how I could be a better salesman.

I just listened and occasionally repeated something that he said.

When he finished, I thanked him, mentioned some good points he'd made, and committed myself to taking his advice.

When I did that he looked at me and just beamed. Like he'd just been given a Nobel Prize for wisdom.

The next time I went back he was a different person. Warm and friendly, he greeted me and wanted to know how I was doing with *his* ideas.

I gave him a report. It wasn't long before it dawned on me that when I called on him I wasn't coming by to sell him anything. I was actually going by to report to him how his ideas were working for me.

It also dawned on me that, in his eyes, he didn't see me as someone who was trying to get him to buy something. Rather, he now saw me as his student.

He liked that. And he liked me too. He began buying from me.

In a couple of years, he moved to a new job. He called me to come by. I had never sold his new firm anything. He took me around and introduced me to the people in the office.

He told them that I was a successful young salesman . . . and that he had taught me everything I knew!

Let me ask you a question. What needs did I fill that caused him to want to buy from me?

How did I know? Because I listened to him.

My point is that people have different kinds of needs. And different people buy for different reasons.

Professional salespeople have, or have developed, the skill of relating to the different styles of buyers. They also understand basic buying motives of different people. They understand them because they've trained themselves to ask questions . . . and to really listen. To listen to the obvious and the not-so obvious.

Hopefully these ideas give you plenty of food for thought.

In Conclusion

My objective is that you not just read these ideas and stories, but that you apply them to your own selling.

Again, it's important that you read this chapter several times this week. The repetition will firmly plant the concepts into your mind. You'll also be motivated more to apply them.

Go back and learn the types of interview questions that you can ask different styles of buyers. Then practice asking them. In your pre-call planning, jot down a few questions that you might ask. Remember to match the questions to the style of the person whom you're contacting.

Don't expect instant mastery. Just ask them as you can comfortably do so. Soon you'll get better . . . and better.

Learning and practicing these concepts can help you increase your selling skills. They can help you have more selling confidence. They can help you have less fear of rejection, and they can also put more dollars in your bank account!

INTEGRITY SELLING
SUCCESS PRINCIPLE

People are more apt to respond to information you ask them for than to information you freely give them!

5

How to Demonstrate What You're Selling

In traditional stimulus/response selling, the sales demonstration is the method used to cause interest, create desire, and sell. In need-fulfillment selling, Demonstration is done only after rapport has been gained and needs or wants identified.

Today, we train people who sell our sales-training programs to make their first call a nondemonstration call. We tell them only to Approach and Interview—to gain rapport and get agreement on needs and *then* schedule a Demonstration call.

If they can't get agreement on needs, there's no reason to schedule a Demonstration call.

Never Begin Selling, Telling, or Demonstrating Until Your Prospect Admits a Need or Desire

I had to learn this the hard way. In 1975 I wrote a six-week course called "Money Plan." Money Plan was designed for the two thirds of American families who don't save on a regular basis. We wanted to sell it to banks to offer to people as a marketing program.

The feedback we got in research was very good. But when we went to market the program, we found very chilly receptions.

I had beautiful presentation panels made up and had purchased special large presentation cases to carry them in.

An associate, Chuck Gregory, and I then began calling on banks to sell the program to them and train in-house people to conduct the weekly sessions for customers.

I've never taken such a beating in my life! Never had I met less interest and more objections!

Together we made over 250 calls on banks before we made a single sale—not even any warm interest. It was devastating.

But as I look back, it was one of the best lessons in selling I ever learned. The lessons I learned paid off many times more than whatever money I would have made if we had sold the program to every bank we called on.

One of the major lessons I learned was to get agreement on need before I demonstrated. Learning that principle has been an extremely profitable lesson to me in the ensuing years.

We'd call a number of banks and make appointments with their marketing or training directors. Of course, this was a mistake, because almost none of them could make a decision on a new program.

Our strategy was to go in, introduce ourselves, and tell

them we had a new program for banks that we'd like to talk to them about.

Usually the people who granted appointments weren't all that busy anyway. We'd begin by showing the program materials and then pull out these large presentation boards.

We bored them to tears! But we did get a new world's record in Dallas, where we called on fifteen to twenty banks. One person held out for a full six minutes before he folded his arms, rolled back his eyeballs, and began reliving the exciting vacation he'd just returned from.

I laugh when I think about it, but I suppose that's how we all learn.

My point is—never begin selling, telling, or demonstrating your product or service until your prospect has sufficiently admitted a need.

The Demonstration Action Guides

Let me stop a moment and mention the action guides for the Demonstration step. They are:

1. Repeat the prospect's dominant wants or needs.
2. Demonstrate the product or service that will answer those wants or needs.
3. Avoid talking about the price. Make it secondary to finding out what best fills the prospect's needs.
4. Ask for the prospect's reactions, feelings, or opinions.

Repeat Prospect's Dominant Wants or Needs

Repeating the customer's or client's wants or needs is the stepping-stone to go from the Interview to your Demonstration.

If I were visiting with your firm about our "Best Seller" video sales-training program, I'd do the Approach and Interview steps. If you admitted a need or interest, I'd then prepare an action plan and come back for a Demonstration. I'd begin by repeating the dominant wants or needs that we'd agreed upon. I might say something like "I'm excited about sharing with you how our Best Seller program can increase your salespeople's sales and positively impact your net profit. . . .

"You told me that you have twenty salespeople and that they've had only product-knowledge training and no actual sales-skills training. You also told me that you have a limited budget but that your salesperson turnover is higher than you want it to be.

"Based on these needs that you've shared with me," I'd go on, "let me share with you a cost-effective, yet result-oriented, program."

After saying this I'd begin my actual, physical Demonstration. I'd show the training kit, the components, the instructor's guide, explain the session format and weekly follow-ups. I'd show the student learning aids, wall posters, and videotapes. If appropriate, I'd show a demonstration video that explained the program.

Your Demonstration Should Help People Visualize the End-Result Benefits

Whatever you're selling—whether it's a tangible product, a service, or an idea—your Demonstration should help your prospect visualize the desired end-result benefits.

In other words it's not enough for them just to understand *what* you're selling; they must understand what benefits they'll enjoy from it. We'll talk more about this in the Validation step, but I mention it here to set the stage to understand a very important sales principle.

Demonstrate the Product or Service That Will Answer Wants or Needs

Let me say it again: *The purpose of a sales demonstration isn't just for your prospect to understand* what *you're selling! The purpose is for them to visualize the* end-result benefits—how it will satisfy their wants or needs.

Stop a moment and mull over this principle.

This is a powerful principle that most salespeople don't know about . . . or at least most don't practice it. If you don't believe me, carefully notice the next ten people who try to sell you something. Notice what their objective is during their demonstration. You'll see that it's usually to tell you about what they're selling, not to help you visualize the *end-result benefits.*

Now, while I'm throwing out miscellaneous ideas, let me lay another one on you, one so simple that you'll say, "I should have known that already!" But observe salespeople and you'll see that not everyone follows it.

Recently I was visiting my friend Gerhard Gschwandtner,

publisher of *Personal Selling Power*. In our conversation, he shared this concept with me:

> In your demonstration, when you mention product or service features, look and point to the *feature*. But when you mention the corresponding benefit, look at the *person*.

Simple isn't it? But as I said, I'd never thought of that before.

Mention Only the Features and Benefits That Appeal to Your Prospect

Another tip, and one that most salespeople don't know, is to mention only the features and benefits that relate to the needs or wants that have been identified.

I bought a videocassette recorder recently, and I thought I was going to have to tape the salesperson's mouth shut. He wanted to tell me everything he knew about the VCR. How it was made, how you fiddle with all those knobs and buttons . . . all the technology.

I didn't want to know everything he wanted to tell me. All I wanted to know was "is this a good one?" and "how do I put a tape in and make it work?"

That's all I wanted to know!

The salesman hadn't been trained to find out my needs or wants and then tailor his demonstration to fit them.

Think about this concept, and you'll see that you can use it almost every day in your selling life. You'll also begin to analyze the selling style of salespeople you meet, and you'll be amazed at how little most of them really know about selling.

Avoid Talking About Price—
Make It Secondary to Finding Out
What Best Fills Their Needs

The third action guide is: Avoid talking about price. Make it secondary to finding out what best fills your prospect's needs.

Here's another sales suggestion that can make you lots of money.

How many times do you get premature price questions? By premature price questions, I mean how often do prospects ask you "how much is it?" before you're ready to talk about the price?

When Is the Right Time to Talk About Price?

This brings up another important point: When *is* the right time to talk about the price?

The right time to talk about the price is when you think your prospect will see that the value exceeds the cost.

Think about that for a moment. The right time to talk about the price is when you think your prospect will see that the value exceeds the cost.

You see, before we make a buying decision, we all compare the value with the cost.

Think of it as a balance-beam scale—when you put something on one side, that side goes down and the opposite side goes up.

We all weigh the cost against the value before making a buying decision.

The cost includes such things as money, time, commitment, risk, trouble, and other considerations.

"The Price Isn't Important . . . Until People Find What They Want!"

An old pro gave me some very good advice many years ago when I owned a retail furniture store. He said, "The price isn't important . . . until people find what they want."

I never forgot that. He was right, too. The price isn't important until your customers find what they want or need.

But, let's face it. Premature price questions are very common, aren't they?

How to Deal with Premature Price Questions

Let me give you a strategy for dealing with premature price questions. It's helped many people make lots of sales and earn lots of money they wouldn't have otherwise enjoyed.

I'll mention these in general terms. You'll understand the principles involved and be able to reword this response to fit your own selling situation.

Let's assume that someone asks you prematurely, "How much does it cost?" Your response might be:

> *I appreciate your concern about the cost. I know it's very important and you want the best price possible . . .* (Argue their case for them—tell them why they should be concerned.) *. . . But before I can quote you an exact cost, there's some more information I need to have . . .* (Then immediately ask for the information.)

Stop and think for a moment and you'll see that this response is often true and will fit many of your premature price questions.

Here's another way to handle when someone asks, "How much does it cost?" Another response might be:

> I appreciate your concern for the cost. I know it's very important and you want the best price possible.
>
> But, before we even *think* about the price, let's make sure we've selected the right thing to fill your needs.

Now, again, if you stop and reread these two responses to premature price questions, you'll see that they fit many of your selling situations. Many times when someone asks you, "How much does it cost?" and you give one of these responses, you'd be telling the truth. And when you tell the truth they usually believe you.

I encourage you to learn these two responses and be able to respond with them automatically whenever you get a premature price question.

Another way to deal with premature price questions is to answer a question with a question. When someone asks, "How much is it?" answer, "What general price range are you thinking about?"

There are few techniques suggested in this chapter that can be used more than these. They can be a valuable resource for you—when used out of an integrity base.

In your Demonstration step, there comes a time when you must mention the price or cost. Remember I said that "cost" includes several things besides just the price. It can include the risk of buying, the time or trouble the purchase will present, or the hassle of implementing.

How to Present the Price

When it's the time to present the price or cost, here are some tips for doing that:

1. Look into your prospect's eyes.
2. Say the price or cost as if it were worth ten times what you're asking. (You can say it like it's ten times what you're asking when you really believe it is!)
3. Then translate the price or cost into value:
   a. Reduce to cost per day, per week, or per month
   b. Show return on investment
   c. Compare with what they're spending now
   d. Show the savings
   e. Mention joy, comfort, or pride of having your offering.

I watched a pro sell a television once . . . and I've never forgotten it.

When it came time to present the price, here's how he did it:

He looked squarely at his prospect and said, "The price of this television set is $750 [I've forgotten the actual price, but let's assume it was $750], which may sound like a lot of money . . . until you stop and consider that it'll probably last you fifteen years.

"And if it lasts you fifteen years," he went on, "that means it'll only cost you about fifty dollars a year to own it.

"Now what that means is that for only about a dollar a week you can enjoy this beautiful twenty-four inch color set in your home.

"So the real question," he went on, "isn't how much does it cost? The real question is, 'Is it worth a dollar a week for you to enjoy this beautiful color television and for your family and neighbors to come into your home and enjoy it with you?'

"*That's* the real question!" he concluded.

As I said, I thought that was a classic.

Other Suggestions to Help Make
Your Demonstrations Effective

Here are some more suggestions that will help you make your sales demonstrations more effective:

1. Get your prospects involved in your demonstration. Get them doing activities, holding things for you, and helping you.
2. Appeal to both their logic and their emotions. Remember that *you sell people with logic, but they buy out of emotion.* Emotions include how it will make them look, feel, or be recognized, or how it will appeal to their pride, profit, pleasure, or peace of mind.
3. Position yourself correctly. Watch how close people want you to get to them. Don't invade their space. Only get as close as they want you to get.
4. Choose the best environment. Get prospects in isolated places—not in places where interruptions will occur.

Get People Involved in Your Demonstrations

Every time I think about the power of getting people involved in demonstrations, I remember an event that happened in the early sixties.

My wife and I were invited over to some friend's home for a cookware party. That was the last thing I wanted to do. It was a situation that we couldn't gracefully get out of, though. I agreed to go, but I didn't agree either to enjoy it or to act nice.

As it turned out, however, it was a productive evening for many reasons.

When we arrived there, I saw one of the most stumbling, fumbling people I'd ever seen before. This guy had almost no confidence. He dropped lids, misplaced food items, and apologized every time he turned around. He was one of the most insecure people I'd ever seen.

At first I was incensed about having to spend an evening like this. But then a very interesting thing happened. It became so obvious that this salesman was going to have a tough time putting everything together that, without anyone being conscious of it, we all pitched in and helped. He showed his gratitude very openly. Within a few minutes, he was orchestrating the whole show and we were doing all the work.

It was hilarious!

Whether he realized it or not, he had us selling ourselves. He showed us how his stainless-steel pans were so strong that they'd ruin an aluminum pan when banged together. Of course, he didn't do the banging. We were afraid to let him. So one of us did.

He also got one of the wives scrubbing an aluminum pan with steel wool—to show the grey, yucky color that resulted. All of us gagged at having something like that going into our stomachs. We all praised the meal he'd "fixed" for us—afraid that if we didn't his self-esteem would suffer more damage.

When he got to the end of the meeting, his close was pathetic. He could hardly explain how to fill out the order form. Finally we had to look at it, decide what went where, and "help" him figure it out.

Of course we all bought! We couldn't have lived with ourselves if we'd rejected such a weak person! It would've been like stomping a baby chicken, or running down a grandmother!

A few days later when he delivered our set, I asked him how many of the people there bought.

"Oh, everyone," he responded. "All five couples."

"Well, how many of these meetings do you hold each week?" I asked him.

He appeared to be reluctant to have to admit how few he held, explaining that he wasn't doing as well as he should, he had some past-due bills to pay off, and he needed a better car.

"Only about three a week," he said, fumbling with the delivery receipt, trying to figure out which one he left with me. Like a mother hen, I helped him out when he asked if I could figure out which one he should leave me. Thanking me, he left.

After he left, I got to figuring out how much he made. "On a $450 sale, he's bound to make $100 commission. He sold five sets the other night. That's . . . $500. He does this three times a week. That's . . . $1,500 per week times four. Great day! That's $6,000 per month. That's more than I make in my furniture store! And I've got a big investment!"

In Conclusion

In order to assimilate and apply these ideas in your sales demonstrations, please follow these suggestions:

1. Write these four action guides on an index card.
   - Repeat the prospect's dominant wants or needs.
   - Demonstrate the product or service that will answer those wants or needs.
   - Avoid talking about the price. Make it secondary to finding out what best fills the prospect's needs.

  • Ask for the prospect's reactions, feelings, or
    opinions.
2. Carry this card with you all this week and put
   the action guides into practice as often as possible.
3. Reread this chapter several times this week and
   relate it to your selling.

Remember: Demonstrate only after a person has admitted
wants or needs to you. And then show and tell only the
features and benefits that fit the needs or wants that have
been identified.

Carefully follow these suggestions and you'll increase the
frequency you take deposit slips to the bank!

INTEGRITY SELLING
SUCCESS PRINCIPLE

**People are more apt to buy when you communicate
end-result benefits than when you communicate only
the product or service features!**

6

How to Demonstrate to Different Styles of Buyers

In your Demonstration you show how your product or service will fill the wants or needs that your prospect has admitted. I said "admitted," because unless a person admits a need, there's usually no reason to demonstrate.

When you do demonstrate, it's important to deliver a demonstration consistent with your customer's buying style.

Different people demand different types of information, so you must demonstrate your product or service in different ways to different kinds of people.

Recently my wife took one of our grandsons up to our mountain cabin. In the process she got into a rainstorm. The dirt road was very muddy, and she got stuck for what seemed to be an eternity.

She wasn't very thrilled about this happening and made it

clear that if I had any kind feeling for our grandchildren and grandchildren-to-come, I should provide a more suitable vehicle for muddy mountain roads.

After listening to her for another eternity, my logic took over and I had a sudden flash of inspiration that it would be a terrific idea if we invested in a four-wheel-drive vehicle.

So the next week, when I had a day in town, I decided to go out and get a Chevrolet Blazer.

I went to the local Chevy dealer and went straight to Charley Conley's office. Charley is an old friend and the new truck sales manager.

"Charley . . . how quick can you sell me a new Blazer?"

Looking at me and grinning, he replied, "Oh, it'll take about thirty seconds."

"You're on . . . let's look at 'em."

"What color do you want?"

"Red."

"What do you want on it?"

"I don't care. Whatever a red one *has* on it!"

Taking me out to look at the Blazers, where he had ten to fifteen all lined up, he said, "See any you like?"

"No, I want a red one."

"The only red one I have is a demonstrator."

"How many miles on it?"

"I don't know . . . let's go see."

So we found the red one. He looked and said, "It's got seven hundred miles on it. You want to drive it?"

"Sure."

"Get in," he pointed.

We both got in and I drove it around the block.

"Don't you want to drive it longer?" he asked.

"No, I'm in a hurry."

Then we went into his office.

"What's it going to cost me?" I asked.

"Let me look." Just then Dub Bragg, the general sales

manager came by. "Hey Dub, how much can we let Ron have this Blazer for?"

Dub looked at the book, mumbled, rolled his eyes, and spit out a figure.

"Is that a good deal?" I asked Charley.

"Yeah, it's a good deal," he replied.

"Sounds good to me," I replied. "I'll call you in thirty minutes."

I turned around and was leaving.

"Hey, Charley, stop him and tell him about all the options on it," Dub advised, obviously thinking I was probably shopping around.

So, Charley called me back and started going over all the options.

"Don't bother me with all that," I said. "All I want to know is how much it is and does it have four-wheel drive."

"Of course it does," he responded. "You want me to show you how it works?"

"No, man, I'm in a hurry . . . I can figure it out by myself if I ever use it . . . I'll call you in a few minutes."

I left him puzzled and went back to my office.

Then, after about twenty-five minutes, sufficient time to make a decision, I called him and asked when he could have it ready.

That's the way I like to buy things. When I go to buy, I go to buy! I already have my mind made up. I never go to shop around. I don't like to shop around.

But is everyone that way? Of course not! Different styles of buyers buy differently.

I didn't ask Charley but I'm sure he sells cars to all sorts of buyer styles.

Different Styles of Buyers Want Different Types of Information

After I bought the car I was imagining how different buyers would buy it.

My style is that of a Doer. I may take time or I may make a decision quickly. But once a decision has been made I act fast. I want to get it done and go on to something else.

My wife's style is a combination Plodder and Controller. She wants to go over everything with a fine-tooth comb, check every detail, and know every fact and bit of information she could ever possibly need to know.

She'll pick a salesperson to pieces with questions. She'll carefully read all the manuals, and she never fails to send in all the warranty cards. Not only that, but she'll mail them herself, rather than trusting me to do it.

It drives me up the wall to have to bother with details like that, but I need people around me who will.

Demonstrating to a Controller

When you demonstrate your product or service to a Controller, you'd better stress these areas:

1. How your product or service features will promote greater efficiency
2. How your product or service will pay for itself— why it's a good investment
3. How your product or service will logically solve a problem, or prevent problems from occurring.

Controllers are interested in warranties and guarantees. They want questions answered about problems they've heard may exist with your service or product.

When you talk features and benefits, remember Controllers want the benefits of sound investment and greater efficiency. So point out all the features that deliver their kind of benefits.

Demonstrating to Plodders

A Plodder won't buy a car without careful consideration. Then the Plodder would want to know each and every detail about the car—fuel economy, reliability, possible drawbacks, etc.

Plodders would want to test-drive them in several different types of road conditions. They'd want to talk to someone they trust who knows something about cars.

Then they'd shop around for the best deal before they made a decision. They'd understand the warranty. They'd know how many gallons of gas the tank held and how many quarts of oil. They'd also want some explanation of what a V-6 engine is.

They buy only after careful consideration. When they finally buy, it's often after the salesperson has already written them off. And if possible, they buy from salespeople whom they can trust—who display stability, honesty, and integrity.

How to Demonstrate to Talkers

If a Talker went to buy a car you'd see quite a different scene. First of all, Talkers wouldn't go to buy, at least at first; rather they'd go to look . . . and visit.

Talkers would want to know the salesperson's name, how long he'd been at the dealership, and what his grandchildren's names are.

Talkers would want to tell the salesperson about their

own grandchildren and find out who the salesperson knows that they know.

When Talkers begin talking about going skiing in the winter, or pulling a boat to the lake, or taking their friends camping, the salesperson better be listening, because signals are being given off as to the type of buyer he is. Talkers would want to know how other people have enjoyed their Blazer. *Enjoyed* is the key word.

They'd probably be very interested in the color and the options—especially the stereo and tape deck. They'd usually be unhurried—they thoroughly enjoy looking and visiting. Talkers would want you to do a lot of listening, to make them feel important, and to introduce them to important people around your firm.

Talkers and Plodders often relish buying experiences. They often get their kicks shopping around. They string out their Christmas shopping and make a pleasurable, entertaining experience out of it.

Controllers and Doers usually don't get all that much gratification from shopping and buying. Time is too important to them to waste it looking around.

Years ago when I owned a retail furniture store I had almost no sales-skills training. No one ever told me that different styles of people buy in different ways. I learned it in a vague way.

I figured out that people who looked at furniture looked through these different glasses:

- Some showed a dominant desire for sturdy construction.
- Some showed a dominant desire for color, form and design.
- Some showed a dominant desire for a good price.
- Others showed a dominant desire for furniture that was like the furniture their friends had.

Analyze these dominant buying motives and you'll see that some were motivated by social reasons, others by artistic reasons, some by utilization reasons, and others by financial reasons.

Had I been analytical enough then to understand these buying motives, I would have clearly seen the four buyer styles of:

Talkers
Doers
Controllers
Plodders

To change the subject slightly, let me say that I realize that not everyone reading this book is selling cars or furniture. I realize that you might be selling computers, software, electronic gadgets, gas masks, or a thousand other things—tangible or intangible.

Learn These Principles . . .
Regardless of What You're Selling

It really doesn't matter what you're selling . . . if you learn these principles of sales communication.

One of the biggest mistakes I see salespeople make is wanting to learn specific *techniques* of selling their product or service—rather than first learning the deeper *principles.*

Techniques of demonstration will land you far short unless you first understand sales principles.

I've said that twice for emphasis.

Here are some more principles of demonstrating your product or service. Carefully read and see if there are a couple of ideas that you can use:

1. Only demonstrate the features, advantages, and benefits that are consistent with the needs that

your prospect has agreed upon. Don't throw every feature in your arsenal at them. You may swamp them.

2. Get your prospects involved. Create an atmosphere in your demonstration in which both of you are sitting down to see if your service or product will satisfy their wants or needs. Don't talk a lot about what your product or service is; rather, talk of end-result benefits. Make sure all your pictures, models, products, drawings, brochures, or whatever you use in your demonstrations cause your prospect's mind to focus on the desired end-result benefit.

4. Pay attention to your prospects' body language. It will tell you about their dominant interests and which of your product's features and benefits are the most desirable.

5. Get them talking about and visualizing the end-result benefits or rewards.

I was visiting with a client company's president recently to talk about an extensive training program for his company.

"What would happen to your company if your sales and service people were more customer-oriented than technology-oriented," I asked him.

He leaned back and began talking. "Well, I suppose we'd increase our market share . . . and quit running off customers, and I suppose we'd increase our business and profits . . . ."

Then for a while we talked (or rather *he* talked) about the end-result benefits. He sold himself. He was ready to accept my recommendation.

Talk in Terms of the End-Result Benefit

I can't stress this principle too much: *talk in terms of the end-result benefit* and make sure you understand the end-result benefit from your prospect's perspective.

So many salespeople don't know how to do this. Watch them if you don't believe me. The next few times you go to buy something, make a special, mental note of this. You'll see that most salespeople talk in terms of what their product or service *is* . . . rather than talking in terms of what it will *do* for their prospects.

Recently I held a "Patient-Centered Selling" seminar for a group of dentists in Palm Beach, Florida. I really hit hard on this concept. I stressed that they weren't in business to do dental procedures . . . that they were in business to help patients look better, feel better, and keep their teeth longer.

After the two-day seminar ended, one doctor, who lived in Palm Beach, invited me to go by and see his office and have dinner.

When we got to his office he showed me around and then took me into his private office. "Many of my friends criticize me for having such a large office," he apologized, "but this is where I sell all my cases."

He then explained to me that he grossed about $80,000 to $90,000 per month after being in practice only four years. He did some very advanced work with implants.

As we were talking he seated me at a square table where he did his case presentations. Immediately he reached out for three binders that had plastic sheet protectors with photographs of work he'd done.

Very dramatically, he took the center book out and pitched it into a wastebasket.

I looked puzzled and surprised, I suppose, because he

said, "What I learned from your seminar caused me to do that."

"What do you mean?"

"When you talked about focusing on the desired end-result benefits during a case presentation, you really hit me where it hurt!"

"Tell me more," I replied.

"Well," he said, reaching into the wastebasket and pulling out the book, "let me show you what I threw away."

He then explained to me that one of the books contained "before pictures" of his patients' mouths. The other book showed the "afters" after receiving dental implants. The book he'd thrown into the wastebasket showed the "during."

He opened it up and showed me all these bloody, gory pictures of patients' mouths during treatment.

"It just dawned on me today that I've been scaring people with these! Yeah, people don't want to see all this 'chopped liver.' They want to see pictures of beautiful mouths."

Well, he'd gotten the message. Focus on the desired end-result benefits, not on the process or product.

Determine the End-Result Benefits from Your Prospect's Perspective

I mentioned that Doers aren't too interested in details or lengthy feature explanations. They want you to tell them what's going to happen.

So be sure to stress bottom-line results to them.

Talkers and Plodders usually want to know more details than Doers. You should spend more time explaining features to them. They'll often be intrigued with certain features and how they work. Often you'll find that analytical engineer types or gadget freaks fall into the Talker/Plodder styles.

They want to know how things work, how they're put together.

When you sense that they fall into these styles, you should plan to spend more time explaining the features of your service or product.

Controllers are often interested in the advantages your service or product has over other competitive ones. Remember . . . they buy out of a logical, functional, efficiency base.

Selling Isn't Just Learning and Applying Techniques

In each of these chapters, I want to repeat one important point. Selling is much more than just learning and applying techniques.

Being concerned only with sales techniques will cause your prospects to feel manipulated.

Again, the techniques I share with you are to be practiced out of an integrity base. How do you do that?

Make Your Selling Integrity Based

Your selling is integrity based when you exhibit these values:

1. Your main motivation is to create value for your customers or clients.
2. You thoroughly understand *their* wants or needs.
3. You don't begin selling, telling, or demonstrating, until your prospects have verbalized and agreed upon their needs or wants.
4. Your attitude sincerely communicates "I'm not here just to sell you something. I'm here to bet-

ter understand your problems, wants, or needs,
in order to see if I can create value for you."

These four values must be clearly communicated by you
to your prospects. If not, try as you will to conceal a manipulative, self-centered attitude, you won't be able to. It'll be
as clear as tracks on fresh snow.

Integrity Selling carries with it its own strong motivation,
persuasion and validation.

In Conclusion

As we end this chapter let me mention these main points
that I want you to remember about demonstrating your
product or service to different styles of buyers.

1. *Talkers want to develop relationships.* They
   want help making decisions. They love to shop
   around and visit. They're interested in how your
   product or service will bring social approval to
   them.
2. *Doers want quick information.* Don't bore them
   with features that excite you but aren't interesting to them. Stress end-result benefits.
3. *Controllers want facts,* data, and proof. They'll
   buy only when they see the logic of your offers.
4. *Plodders are interested in features,* as well as
   benefits. They'll take plenty of time to decide.
   Push them and you've lost them.

Again, please read this message several times this week.
This will help you *recognize, relate, assimilate,* and *apply*
these principles.

Follow these suggestions as you demonstrate your product or service to different styles of buyers.

When you program these concepts into your unconscious
mind through repetition, you'll begin to practice them automatically in your selling.

INTEGRITY SELLING
SUCCESS PRINCIPLE

People are more apt to understand your offering when they experience it, than when they just hear about it!

7

How to Validate Your Claims

Before you can expect people to buy from you, they must believe your claims, but even more important, they must first believe *you!*

Many sales are lost because the prospect or customer didn't genuinely believe the salesperson's claims or didn't trust the salesperson.

In other words the salesperson didn't validate his or her claims. He or she didn't communicate integrity!

Not long ago, we did a survey prior to a sales-training project for a client who sells a product that all of you would recognize.

In surveying their customers we found that they rated the skills of the salespeople who called on them only 28 percent on a 100-percent scale in the area of compatibility and only 40 percent in trust and rapport.

A pretty significant discrepancy, isn't it?

These salespeople's bosses rated them almost identically

to the customers' rating. I think this survey revealed a pretty common reality. Customers see salespeople differently than salespeople see themselves.

In the same survey we measured selling pressure, which of course is a negative selling skill.

In selling pressure, the salespeople rated themselves about 65 percent, their customers rated them just over 80 percent, and their superiors rated them just over 40 percent.

That was really interesting!

What that says is that customers rated them low in trust, rapport, and compatibility, but high in the negative skill of selling pressure, while at the same time their superiors thought they applied a rather low amount of selling pressure.

Where Trust and Rapport Are High, Selling Pressure Is Perceived Low

One of my beliefs as a sales trainer is that where trust and rapport are strong, selling pressure will usually appear weak—regardless of how strong it really is.

Think of that a moment.

Said another way . . . where trust and rapport are weak, any selling pressure will appear strong and will have a negative impact upon sales.

Understand these points and a lot of confusion about selling pressure will be cleared up.

Now, as we continue our message on Validation, let me also mention that Validation isn't necessarily a separate step in the AID, Inc. system. It's an ongoing process.

We Validate from beginning to end. We Validate by who we are, how we package ourselves, and how we present ourselves.

Before You Can Successfully Negotiate
and Close, You Must First Validate

Let me say again that Validation isn't a separate step, but an ongoing process. The reason we put it where it is in the AID, Inc. system is that before we can successfully Negotiate and Close we must first have Validated.

In fact, many sales fall apart because sales people attempt to negotiate and close before they Validate themselves and their product or service.

Reflect upon your own experience in selling and I'll bet you'll agree with this statement.

Not long ago a man called my office several times wanting to come in to see me. He explained that he'd read my book *The Best Seller* and wanted to ask me some questions.

Finally, after his fifth or sixth call, my assistant pleaded with me to see him. "Tell him I charge $150 an hour for office consultation," I told her.

Well, a week or so later he called again. She told him the fee and he said, "OK, that's fine."

So she scheduled an appointment from ten to noon one morning.

"What does he sell?" I asked her.

"He's a siding salesman," she replied.

When the day arrived for his appointment I met one of the worst-kempt people I'd ever seen.

His hair was thick, bushy, and red. He hadn't had a haircut in eons. He had on some old jogging shoes that looked awful. He had on blue jeans that were so old that one of the rear pockets was half-ripped off. His knit T-shirt should've been a size larger, and the pack of cigarettes that was in his shirt pocket stuck out noticeably.

He reeked of cigarette smoke. He opened his mouth and I saw a mouthful of teeth that were in the process of rotting.

Not only could I *see* them . . . you got it . . . I could also *smell* them!

My first impression was, "No wonder you need help . . . who'd trust someone who presents themselves as you do!" I wouldn't have trusted him if he'd come to sell me siding.

He came into my office, sat down, and laid a copy of my book on my desk. It was very dog-eared and dirty. When he opened it I saw that he'd underlined passages, made notes in margins and had obviously spent a lot of time on it.

Then he began to ask questions. To my surprise they were very intelligent, to-the-point questions. I could tell he'd spent a lot of time preparing them.

Within an hour I became impressed with him and his knowledge of selling, and his desire to improve himself.

At the end of the two hours as he was about to pay me, I said to him, "Chuck, I've made a decision while we've been talking."

He looked at me puzzled, almost afraid to ask what the decision was. Then he said, "What do you mean?"

"I'm impressed with your desire," I went on. "I don't know how much integrity you have or how much character you have. But if you have what it takes, then I'll have made the right decision.

"My decision is that since I believe you're sincerely interested in improving yourself, I'm going to take the money that I've just earned and invest it where I think it'll pay some big dividends."

Still puzzled, he listened.

"I'm going to invest the money that I've just earned . . . in you."

"In me?" he asked.

"Yes, in you. I'm going to invest my $300 in you, and here's how I want you to spend my money.

"I want you to go from here to the barber shop in the shopping center across the interstate and get a haircut.

"Then I want you to go out to this particular men's cloth-

ing store and see Ted Billingsly. Tell him that I sent you and
you want to buy a pair of navy-blue dress slacks and a pair
of tan ones. Also get a couple of button down, short-sleeved
sport shirts.

"Then I want you to go see Dr. Jim Hollifield and ask him
how much it'll cost to fix your teeth. Tell him how much you
have and ask him how you can pay out the balance."

Looking straight at him I asked him, "Will you do that?
Will you spend my money that way?"

"Why are you doing this?" he asked me, looking puzzled.

"Because, despite how you look now, I think I see a better
person in you. I see a person who has a very high desire to
succeed. As I said, I don't know how much integrity you
have, but I know you have desire. If you also have a lot of
integrity and character with your desire, you'll reach whatever sales goals you want to reach.

"If you agree to do this, I want you to come back in thirty
to forty-five days and give me an accounting of how you
spent my money. Then I want to see you again in six
months.

"If you spent my money wisely and can show a profitable
return, I'll invest in you further."

"Invest . . . how?" he asked.

"I'm not sure . . . maybe time, maybe knowledge, maybe
money. I'm not sure. All I'm sure of is that if you can show
me a good return on my investment, I'll invest more."

He thanked me and left.

That's been several months ago now . . . and I wish I
could tell you that it turned out like a story-book adventure.

The fact is that I haven't seen him since, and I suppose I
probably won't.

But I had to make the investment. Whatever happened
later is his problem.

Now, why did I tell you this long-winded story? To emphasize several points:

1. We Validate ourselves by how we look and by how we package ourselves.
2. We influence people when we show strong desire.
3. Our integrity becomes the strongest regulator of our success in selling.

Validation Action Guides

Here are the four action guides that will help you Validate your product or service. Let's think of them for a moment and then discuss each one:

1. Translate product features into customer benefits.
2. Justify the price and emphasize the value.
3. Offer proof-of-benefit and satisfied users.
4. Reassure and reinforce prospects to neutralize their fear of buying.

For a few minutes let's think of these Action Guides. We'll talk about how you can practice them. In the next chapter you'll learn some ways to Validate to different styles of buyers.

Translate Product Features into Customer Benefits

Features are specific points you mention about your offering: 100% wool may be a feature of an article of clothing; solid-state circuitry a feature of a television set; undercoating a feature of an automobile.

Features explain what your service or product is, but benefits are quite different. Benefits are *how* your features will help your customers.

One of the biggest mistakes salespeople make is selling

features instead of benefits. If you don't believe me, watch the next ten people who attempt to sell you something, or watch the next ten people who attempt to sell anyone anything.

Watch them and I'll predict that eight out of the ten will spend a lot more time mentioning features than benefits. They think that selling is telling about their products or services.

To be most persuasive when you're demonstrating your product or service, always make the feature/benefit conversion.

To help you make the feature/benefit conversion, let me share with you a very helpful tool.

Six Magic Words to Help You Validate

The six magic words are: "What this means to you is . . ."

Again: *"What this means to you is . . ."*

The way you use these six magic words is whenever you explain a product or service feature, follow it up with "what this means to you is . . ." and then mention the benefit the person will enjoy or receive—the benefit being the end result: enjoyment, reward, or profit factor.

People don't buy products or services for what they are, they buy them for what they'll *do* for them.

The most basic buying motives are these:

1. People buy for what the service or product will do *for* them.
2. People buy for *how* it will make them look to others.

Memorize the six magic words. Practice using them. Play a little game with yourself—every time you mention a product or service *feature,* follow it with the six magic words, and then follow it by mentioning an end-result benefit.

Justify Price and Emphasize Value

The second action guide is "Justify price and emphasize value." One of the biggest mistakes salespeople make is believing that price is the most important consideration in the prospect's mind. It isn't, but most salespeople are brainwashed into believing it is.

Buyer surveys consistently show that what people really look for isn't price, but value.

Value encompasses several things other than just the price—although price is included in value. Things like length of service, degree of enjoyment delivered, savings realized, warranties included, and pride of ownership.

The first Mercedes I ever bought was in the early sixties, and it cost $5,700. I bought one just the other day and it cost $45,000—a lot of money. But it represented enough value to me to more than offset the cost. I'm sure I could have found the same model cheaper elsewhere, but there's more to its value than the price.

Do all Mercedes salespeople know this? No, they don't! About a month before I bought the one I have I went into a dealer's showroom on Park Avenue in New York City. The salesman asked where I was from and then said, "I can deliver you one for a lot less than you can get it anywhere else."

"How much?" I asked.

He pulled out his card, checked a book and wrote down a figure. He may as well have been selling commodities . . . pounds or bushels of cars. All he sold on was price. He did nothing to develop rapport with me, validate himself, or qualify me.

Buyers brainwash salespeople into believing their primary interest is price. And it's natural for salespeople to get conditioned to believe it. But it's just not the truth.

Buyers aren't mainly interested in price, but they are mainly interested in value. Remember that!

Offer Proof-of-Benefit and Satisfied Users

Another strong way to Validate or cause people to believe you is to offer proof-of-benefit and satisfied users.

Testimonials, reports, research, evidence—all have an impact on causing people to believe you.

The principle is that people will often believe what *others* say about you and your product or service more than they'll believe what *you* say about yourself.

How can you use consumers' statements or third-party testimonials to help validate what you're selling?

Always ask for letters from satisfied customers or clients. Are you strong enough to allow your satisfied customers to say nice things about you to others?

Another technique that I've taught salespeople is to keep a couple of very good reference or testimonial letters in reserve. When and if you have a prospect who needs a slight additional bit of proof, bring the letters or evidence out.

Another way to use this idea is to submit proposals to prospects. If you already sell through proposals, you've probably known many occasions in which the proposal appeared stalled in your prospect's hands awaiting a decision.

In cases like this you have to assume that the longer the proposals sit, the colder they get. Also, the colder the feet of your prospects get—especially if they have to sell the proposal to someone else.

A great idea is to send a letter thanking them and saying something like, "Oh, incidentally, here are a couple of our other satisfied users I forgot to tell you about."

This is called "preponderance of evidence." You want to stack up more evidence to tip the decision scales in your behalf.

Getting updated third-party evidence to use in your selling and creatively seeing how you can use it is always time well spent.

Reassure and Reinforce Prospects to Neutralize Their Fear of Buying

The fourth action guide is "Reassure and reinforce prospects to neutralize their fear of buying."

As salespeople, we have to assume that fear always enters a prospect's mind before commitment to buy.

What kind of fear? Fear of making a mistake. Fear of risk. Fear of not getting the best deal. Fear of making a decision and being wrong.

Let's face it, buying can cause a lot of trauma, especially buying larger items. Rapport and trust are often enhanced when salespeople realize this and give reassurance and reinforcement. I think it's often wise to bring this fear out into the open.

Years ago when I had a furniture store, I'd see people get all excited about purchasing new furniture . . . until it came time to make a decision. At this point they'd often freeze and suddenly find all kinds of excuses for not buying.

While many salespeople push hard at this point, I found that pressure often has a negative effect.

I found it was good to stop and bring fears and risks out into the open. Statements like "I understand you're making a major buying decision. You're going to have this furniture for several years. I can see you're concerned about making the best decision."

I'd give them reassurance that I thought they were making a wise decision and that they'd be happy with it.

Often I'd even say, "If for any reason you're not happy with it when you get it in your home, we'll take it back. You don't have to commit yourself unless you're totally satisfied."

Often, saying this, removing the risk for them, would help them make a positive buying decision.

Some people need reassurance and reinforcement. The more they trust you, the more powerful your reassurance is. That's why I believe it's important to relieve pressure at this point, rather than creating more tension.

Funny, isn't it, how trust and rapport keep popping up as successful sales ingredients?

Let me summarize this chapter by repeating that before you can expect people to buy from you, they must first believe you! They must believe your claims, but more importantly, they must believe you.

When you Validate, you do something that causes your prospects to believe you. Many sales fall apart because the Validation step hasn't been completed.

Again, Validation isn't necessarily a separate step in our selling system; actually it's an ongoing process. But it's something we must do before we can expect to Negotiate and Close.

In Conclusion

Remember, if people don't believe you or believe your claims, you might as well pack up and move on because you're probably not going to make a sale.

Again, the Validation action guides are:

1. Translate product features into customer benefits.
2. Justify the price and emphasize the value.
3. Offer proof-of-benefit and satisfied users.

4. Reassure and reinforce prospects to neutralize fear of buying.

Write these action guides on an index card and carry it all this week. Reread this chapter several times. Notice and be aware of the degree of trust and confidence your prospects have in you and your product or service. Make sure people trust you and believe you before you attempt to Negotiate and Close.

As you practice these action guides and learn the principles in this chapter, you'll move ahead of most other salespeople. You'll move yourself into a special league of Integrity Selling!

INTEGRITY SELLING
SUCCESS PRINCIPLE

People are more apt to believe what others say about you than what you say about yourself!

8

How to Validate Yourself to
Different Styles of Buyers

As a sales trainer, I like to observe salespeople to see what degree of integrity they communicate to their customers or prospects.

Recently, I went with my daughter Becky to four or five auto dealerships looking at cars. I was appalled at some of the slick characters we saw. I didn't trust some of them at all.

I came away from that experience asking myself, "What causes us to feel we can't trust people? What causes us to feel we can trust them? How quickly do we form opinions about people we meet?"

Most of us make pretty quick assumptions about salespeople when we come in contact with them. Whether we're right or wrong, these feelings or perceptions influence our decisions.

Let's turn it around for a moment, look at ourselves and ask, "How do people feel about *us* when we meet them? How do they feel after they've talked to us for a while? How do they feel about us when we make our presentation to them? How do they feel about us when it's time to make a buying decision? And how do they feel about us *after* they've made a buying decision?"

How would you answer these questions?

As you think about these, here's another good one:

"What Are Some Factors That Cause People to Make Assumptions About Us?"

I suppose the obvious answers would include: the way we dress, the way we groom ourselves, the total way we package ourselves, how we talk, our body language, our eye contact, and our tone of voice.

These factors are important. But I think we Validate ourselves at a deeper, more profound level.

It seems to me that we validate by *who* we are. The kind of person you are sends loud and clear signals to people. It communicates on the instinctive or intuitive level, but it communicates.

Feelings, hunches, spur of the moment perceptions cause people to form definite beliefs about us.

This is why integrity, honesty, and genuine concern for your customers and their needs powerfully influence your ability to develop trust with people!

When I get right down to it, *who* I am communicates! Sooner or later most people will get the message about the level of integrity I have. And they often get the message pretty quickly.

So, my answer to the question "How can I cause people

to believe me and trust me?" is *"Be* a person that people can trust and believe in."

That's integrity!

Value-Focused® Selling

Value-Focused selling concentrates on the value that can be created for a client or customer. But if you think for a moment you'll clearly see that different salespeople have different foci.

Value-Focused Selling Profile®

Percentage of Sales People	80%				15%	5%
Central sales focus	Survival focus	Quota focus	Product focus	Income focus	Ego focus	Value focus
Success level	Failure	Surviving	Low	Moderate	High	Extremely high
Self-esteem level	Low	Weak	Fair	Moderate	High	Extremely high
Achievement drive level	Low	Weak	Fair	Moderate	High	Extremely high
Call-reluctance level	Extremely high	High	High	High	Moderate	Low
Trust level	Low	Weak	Fair	Moderate	High	Extremely high

Percentage of Sales People	80%				15%	5%
Time-management level	Low	Weak	Fair	Moderate	High	Extremely high
Job-stability level	Low	Weak	Fair	Moderate	High	Extremely high

© 1985 — SALES COMMUNICATIONS

Notice on the chart that there are several central sales foci of salespeople.

Some focus on survival. The motivation is to go out and sell something so they can eat, or so they can pay their bills that are two months behind. Their whole focus or consciousness is on survival: What or who can I sell so I can make it?

Another focus that some salespeople have is on quota. The focus is to sell just enough to make quota. Often this focus is on minimums. Their objective: How can I sell enough to keep the boss off my back . . . but not so much that my quota will be increased next year?

Still another focus is on the product or service we sell. If this is my focus, I'll probably be excited about the product or service. I'll probably spend a lot of time talking about its features and advantages. With this perspective my vision is limited to the extent that I can't see past the sale of the service or product.

Still another focus is on money: How much money I can earn? The motivation here is strictly for their own gain.

With the ego focus, the objective is to outsell other people —either competitors or other associates—to be number one, to win contests, to achieve recognition.

The last focus I'll mention is the value focus. With the value focus, my motivation is to create value for my clients or customer: to increase their profits, productivity, enjoyment, pleasures, etc.

Again, the different focuses are: survival, quota, product or service, money, ego, and value.

Only with the value focus do I identify the prospects' wants or needs. I see things from their perspective. I get into their skin—see things through their eyes.

When You Create High Value for People, You'll Be Highly Rewarded

My philosophy is that if I can create value for people then I'll be rewarded. When I create high value for you, I'll be rewarded highly.

In Value-Focused selling I realize that it's only by creating value for customers that I can be highly compensated. Far from an altruistically weak mind-set, it becomes a realistic, bottom-line producing, personal success direction. In this selling mode, I find that my compensation rises and falls with the value I create for others.

I discover that it's okay to make a lot of money when creating lots of value for others. In fact I come to believe that I *should* make a lot of money . . . as long as I create a lot of value for people.

It's in this level of selling that self-esteem rises to its height; that integrity blossoms; that respect, trust, compatibility, and confidence become the by-products.

Notice again, the Value-Focused selling scale you looked at a moment ago. Notice how your selling skills and attitudes are influenced by the focus you have.

Get that picture in mind and you'll then see that success and income rise as you move toward Value-Focused selling. So does self-esteem, and professionalism, and trust and rapport. And the turnover stability factor. You can plot other realities on this scale.

Then, as you look at this scale, you'll notice that 80 percent of salespeople move from failure to moderate success. The next 15 percent represent a reasonably high degree of success. The far right 5 percent will represent extremely high success levels.

The main point is that as we focus on creating value for customers, we'll be pulled from left to right: From failure to success. From low income to high income. From low self-esteem to high self-esteem. From low trust to high trust.

Dwell on this concept and you'll discover some profound lessons in Validation.

So, again, my point is that people, *regardless* of their behavior style, believe us and trust us when they feel good about us. When they see in us a sincere desire to create value for them.

Buyers Must See Congruence in Us!

The second major point I want to make in this message is that whatever style of buyer we're selling, we must appear *congruent* to that person.

The word congruence means a state of agreement or harmony. When we are in congruence with a prospect, we're in harmony or agreement with that person—emotionally.

We achieve congruence when we *sincerely* communicate with another person in a manner consistent with his or her style.

Read the preceding statement again because it suggests a very profound principle of high-integrity Validation. It suggests that relating to buyer styles isn't just a technique, but a value we have.

Not just a *technique* . . . but a *value!*

Let me pause a moment and reiterate that it's best to analyze, plan, and role-play fitting your validation to your buyers' styles *before* and *after* you're in front of them.

While you're in front of them, you should be totally plugged into them. Totally listening. Totally observing their body language, words, tone of voice, and environment.

To attempt to analyze their buying style while selling to them may cause preoccupation and keep you from really hearing them.

Reacting to buyer styles should be an automatic response. While we're in front of people, we should really listen. We shouldn't try to analyze and figure out their style.

Remember, inspect, analyze, and learn *before* and *after* you meet with your contacts. That'll prepare you to react unconsciously to different styles.

And remember: When you're in front of someone, don't analyze, just listen, care, and feel.

Different Buyer Styles Require Different Benefits

When you translate product or service features into customer benefits, remember that different styles require different benefits.

In your Interview you find out the specific benefits a person wants. Until you know their particular wants or needs, you haven't finished your Interview.

In your Demonstration you present these benefits carefully, getting feedback, or asking for your prospect's feelings or opinions.

Quickly, here are the different types of benefits the different styles will require.

What Benefits Talkers Want

Talkers will want you to prove to them how your product or service will provide enjoyment. How it will make others happy. How it will cause the Talker to receive recognition or appreciation from other people, or allow them to be in the spotlight.

Talkers need to know that you'll be around to follow up and support them: that you'll get them off the hook if problems arise.

What Benefits Doers Want

Doers are very end-result benefit oriented. They'll generally not be as interested in the features as they are in the product or service benefits. They'll want to know clearly and specifically, "What's going to happen? How is this going to profit me? What will the results be? What's the bottom line?"

Doers don't want generalities. They want specifics. So, fire end-result benefit bullets at them.

Doers are generally much more interested in value than price.

What Benefits Controllers Want

Controllers are quicker to pick up on your integrity level than the others. Usually, they're analytical, which means they'll be more critical of you and your product or service.

Like Doers they want quick answers and result-oriented benefits. Controllers also want you to be brief and to the point. But for a different reason: They're no-nonsense people, and they live in a world of logic and facts.

You can strengthen your Validation to Controllers by bringing up possible objections and potential risks before they bring them up. In your presentations bring up the dangers, risks, and possible problems along with your feature and benefit explanations.

Controllers respect people who look at all the angles of a

deal. They also cut you off when they think you're making commitments that might be difficult to keep—or when they think you might be overstating the benefits or exaggerating claims.

Controllers don't like to be pushed either. You can often cause them to move faster when you take pressure off them —when you let them know that you realize they need to make sure they have sufficient information before they make a decision.

In other words, selling pressure has a reverse effect upon them. Controllers often operate under time pressure, but the pressure is always imposed by themselves. So, let them set deadlines. When they make deadline commitments to you, they'll usually keep them.

Controllers will be influenced more by the value than price. They don't mind spending money as long as they see good return on investment. And, more than any other style, they know when they're either getting or not getting the truth.

Their greatest fear is that of making mistakes or being wrong. You must remember this fact as you Validate to them. You must reduce their risks. You must present proof— logical, objective proof.

What Benefits Plodders Want

Plodders want lots of answers to their many questions. Unless they totally trust you, they'll be indecisive.

Plodders aren't pioneers, trailblazers, or innovators. So, you'll turn them on by talking about tried and true things. New and untried things present risks they don't want to take. You'll turn them off by talking about having the newest and best.

Selling pressure will also have a negative effect upon Plodders. It'll cause them to shy away and be indecisive.

Give Plodders plenty of proof—not necessarily proof your service or product works, but proof that the risk is minimized.

They'll trust you more when you take time to visit with them. Talk to them about their families, their lives, or their interests. They'll trust you when they see stability and integrity in you.

Plodders will often be influenced more by price than by overall value. They'll want a thorough explanation of the features before making a decision. They're more feature-oriented than the others.

Direct Evidence Consistent with Your Buyer's Style

Now, another important fact about Validation is that different styles of buyers react best to third-party evidence from their own styles.

Think about that for a moment: *People are influenced more by people of their own style.*

Several years ago, my friend Bernard Petty was selling a nine-week course I'd written. He'd conducted several courses in banks and had enjoyed some very good results.

He called on a bank president who was steely-eyed and unemotional—an obvious Controller. This man showed no signs that resembled the word "positive." Arms folded, jaw set, he just sat and listened.

In a few minutes my friend pulled out a letter he'd received from another bank president and handed it to this prospect. The banker took it, read it carefully, and said in a very unemotional way, "Your program is a good one _ _ _ _ if Weldon Jones says it is."

That sold him. It Validated the course because he respected the person who said it.

About five years after I went into the training field, I was visiting with a good friend who worked for a finance company. He was dissatisfied with his job and was looking around for another field to get into.

I was all fired up about the training business and immediately assumed he would be, too. All of a sudden I could see him doing what I did—getting out of his business and running my training courses.

Within a couple of minutes of thinking about this, I got so fired up that I was ready for him to quit his job, move to another city, and begin marketing my courses.

When I laid this exciting plan on him, it was like I'd questioned his mother's honor.

He shot back, "What do you mean?"

Before I could respond he went on, "You don't expect me to do a dumb thing like you did, and jump out and start doing something without any guarantees or salary?"

He was indignant! And I couldn't for the life of me understand why he didn't jump at the chance to do such an exciting thing as I had.

The truth was that he'd never taken a risk in his life. His mother always told him, "Get a good education and go with a big company where you'll be secure."

He's been in banking for many years now.

I didn't make a sale and at the time didn't have any idea why. Had I understood his Controller/Plodder buying style, I would have understood his actions.

Make Buying What You're Selling Consistent with Who Your Buyers Perceive Themselves to Be

Several years ago a friend told me this story. A successful businessman, he'd gone to his dentist, who recommended about $6,000 worth of work done.

Although my friend could afford it, it wasn't exactly in his value system to spend $6,000 on his mouth.

He told the doctor this and asked if there wasn't a much less expensive method of treating the problem.

The dentist, being pretty astute, replied, "Well . . . yes there is." He paused a moment and then went on, "But this is the one I'd recommend for someone who's achieved your level of success!"

It then took my friend about thirteen seconds to reconsider and accept the doctor's full recommendation.

You see, where before the doctor hadn't exactly communicated in a way consistent with my friend's value system, he later did. And so the sale was made, because this professional was able to Validate to the style of my friend.

This brings up an important principle to remember about Validating, or causing your prospects to believe you and accept what you're telling them. The principle is this: What you present must *appear* to be *consistent* with the *values* of your prospects. It must be consistent with how they perceive themselves and what they think is right for them.

Remember this principle of consistency, which, of course, has a great deal to do with the word introduced before— congruence. *Congruence* means that regardless of your style or your buyers' styles, they must see you and your offering being in harmony or agreement with their wants or needs.

The AID, Inc. System Helps You Achieve Congruence

Stop and think about these points and you'll see how the AID, Inc. system helps you achieve congruence or consistency, and why it's a road map for Integrity Selling.

Your integrity is communicated to people by the statements you unconsciously make when you Approach to gain rapport. When you Interview to identify their wants or needs. When you Demonstrate to show how you can fill or satisfy their wants or needs. When you Validate, or cause

them to believe you and your claims. When you Negotiate a
win-win solution to their problems. When you ask them to
buy.

Yes, in all these steps, your integrity is demonstrated. It's
also shown in Value-Focused selling. When your motivation
isn't just to make a sale, but to create value for your clients
or customers—you show integrity.

Think of these unique selling philosophies and you'll see
that they form a very distinct value system. Selling isn't all
technique . . . it's about having a strong value system!

Integrity.

High ethics.

My belief is that when we actually have these values, our
actions or sales performance will be an extension of them.
We perform consistent with who we are. It's cause and effect.

I've spent a lot of time in this book talking about buyer
styles and how you relate to them. But, frankly, I think
there's a danger in being overly concerned with identifying
buyer styles.

The trap is that we become so concerned with style that
we don't really listen and develop empathy with people.
Then our selling becomes technique-based, not principle-
based and value-focused.

In Conclusion

Applying techniques can be manipulative unless they're
grounded in integrity. We need a balance.

Here's how to achieve that balance:

1. Read this chapter several times this week.
2. After you call on people, analyze their styles.
   Role-play how you could have interacted better.

Role-play what you could have said, or what you did say, that would have communicated better with that person's style.

3. Then, when you contact people forget styles, plug in, and really listen. Listen to their words, tone of voice, and body language. And as you listen, reflect back to them the tone, the level, and the behavior that they display.

4. Then present your Validation in a manner consistent with the way they think.

Follow these simple suggestions, and you'll begin to react in an instinctive, natural way to whatever type of person you're selling.

All your actions will be firmly based in integrity—as you genuinely try to create value for people, you'll achieve an inner congruence. Your congruence will be evident to the people you contact, and you'll be far more successful than you'd otherwise be!

INTEGRITY SELLING
SUCCESS PRINCIPLE

People are more apt to believe you when they see a congruence between what you say and who you are!

9

How to Negotiate Problems and Objections

In Value-Focused selling we view "integrity negotiation" as identifying problems or objections and then working through to a "win-win solution"—a solution where both sides win.

Tricky negotiation strategies aren't consistent with Integrity Selling.

Rather than manipulating, negotiating is determining the roadblocks that keep your prospects from buying, and then removing them. It's creative problem-solving.

We don't view Negotiation as manipulation. We don't see it as outtalking, outsmarting, or outmaneuvering people. We don't view it as combat or as an adversarial relationship.

Instead we view negotiating as a win-win activity—where seller and buyer sit down together and attempt to work out the best solution for both sides.

The salesperson's approach of integrity negotiation creates value for both sides.

And, as you can see, this rules out tricky or gimmicky words, phrases, or strategies.

Several years ago I sold the copyrights and inventory of a program I'd written to another training firm for $250,000. The terms were $25,000 down and $25,000 each six months until the whole amount was paid.

Since the firm had a fairly low net worth and the president had a very high net worth, we agreed that he'd sign the contract both as president of the firm and as an individual.

When I got the contract back, along with the down payment, it wasn't signed on the line labeled "Individually."

When I called the man, he explained that after thinking it over, he didn't want to be personally liable.

I reminded him that those weren't the terms that we'd agreed upon and asked him to pick me up at the airport in his city the next day.

So the next day he met me and again explained that he didn't want the personal liability. He explained that should something happen to him, he didn't want his wife or family to shoulder the burden.

I told him that I could certainly appreciate how he felt— that if I were in his shoes I'd also be concerned.

Then I asked him if that was his only concern or reason for not signing the contract personally. He said, "Yes, that's the only reason."

I explained that without his personal guarantee my bank wouldn't accept collateral should I need to borrow against his contract, which I would do in expanding my business.

Then I asked him if I could guarantee that his wife or estate wouldn't be stuck with the liability should he die an untimely death, would he go ahead and sign the contract as we'd agreed?

"Yes," he said, "if I can be guaranteed of that."

Anticipating this, I had with me an application for a term

insurance policy for $250,000. I gave this to him and told him that I'd pay the premiums for the term of his note.

He was immediately relieved and signed the contract.

The negotiation solved his problem and my problem. It was a reasonable concession for me to make. It left his ego intact and helped him retain his integrity.

We were both happy. It made a win-win situation.

That's what integrity negotiation is!

Negotiation Action Guides

With that in mind, let me mention the action guides for the Negotiation step. They are:

1. Ask, "Is there anything that's keeping you from making a decision now?"
2. Welcome objections—let prospects know that you understand how they feel.
3. Identify specific objections—get agreement that these are the only ones.
4. Discuss possible solutions—ask prospects' opinions for best solutions.

For a few moments let's think of these Action Guides and how you might be able to use them.

To Identify the Problem to Be Negotiated . . . Ask!

The first step in successful negotiation is to identify the problem. And the best way to identify the problem is to ask. Just ask!

How you ask, or the exact words you use, isn't as important as your reason for asking. If your reason is to find out the problem, objection, or roadblock so you can understand it from their viewpoint, then you'll ask right.

And if your sincere objective is to find out so you can work to a win-win solution, you'll also ask right.

I think it's much more important to examine and teach motives rather than specific strategies. Techniques or strategies are only effective if they come out of an integrity base.

Now you'd probably not use the exact words, "Is there anything that's keeping you from making a decision now?" These words are more to explain what to do than what to say. There are other indirect ways to ask.

Here are a few:

> "What other information will you need before making a decision?"
> "What other considerations will you want to think about before going ahead?"
> "What are some other concerns you have that we need to talk about?"
> "What other questions do you have that need to be answered before you feel comfortable making a decision?"

These and other questions can bring out problems or objections that your prospects might have.

Again, it isn't so important *what* you ask as *how* you ask it. Your true motives will influence your tone of voice and will then communicate certain feelings to the other person.

A common weakness that many salespeople have is that of not wanting to know what the real objections, obstacles, or problems are. They don't want to know because they view them as being negative. So often they try to sidestep the truth or sweep it under the rug.

Have the Courage to Face the Truth

One of the most helpful affirmations that I learned from
W. Clement Stone was the one that says, "Have the courage to face the truth!"

I've repeated that affirmation over and over to myself
many times. "Have the courage to face the truth . . . the
courage to face the truth . . . the courage to face the truth."

Repeating that self-suggestion over and over programmed
it into my mind. Now that the programming has been done,
every time I find myself in a situation where I'm reluctant to
ask because I'm afraid of getting a negative response, I unconsciously say to myself, "Have the courage to face the
truth!"

That motivates me to go ahead and find out what problems or objections or negative responses my prospects
have.

You might like to memorize the self-suggestion, "Have the
courage to face the truth!"

Say it to yourself fifty times each morning and fifty times
each afternoon. Do this for several days in a row. This will
permanently program the concept into your unconscious
mind.

Then every time you get in a situation where you need
that reminder, your subconscious will autosuggest, "Have
the courage to face the truth!" to your conscious mind.

When that happens, act immediately.

Let me stop and emphasize that this practice of self-suggestion has had a significant impact upon my confidence
and self-esteem.

So, again . . . it's important to ask your prospects, "Is
there anything keeping you from making a decision now?"

Then when they give you objections, problems, or negative responses, remember to practice the second action guide:

Welcome Objections—Let Prospects Know That You Understand How They Feel

It's at this point that many sales are saved or lost.

Many are lost because the moment we get a negative response, we have an urge to get combative or argumentative: to prove the person's objections aren't valid.

It's here our egos surface and influence the situation negatively.

Many salespeople, by nature, have high ego drives. Without ego drive, which is achievement drive, there isn't the motivation to get out into the cold, cruel world and risk getting your face pushed in. For successful salespeople the thrill of making a sale is stronger than the fear of rejection or failure.

Points Where Fear of Rejection Occurs

I suppose there are three major points where fear of rejection occurs the strongest. They are:

1. In approaching or calling on people
2. In finding out what their objections are
3. In asking for a decision

The ability to respond positively to objections is a real sign of a salesperson's maturity.

The best way to respond is to listen. Just listen. Thoroughly listen. This means always let the person finish talking.

Then, after you have thoroughly listened, let them know that you understand how they feel.

To do this let me present to you the single most important tool that I've ever learned about negotiation. It's called the "feel-felt-found formula." You can use the feel-felt-found formula whenever you get an objection as a negative response.

The Feel-Felt-Found Formula

Suppose you get a negative response and someone says, "I like this, but it's too much money!"

To use the feel-felt-found formula you might respond like this: "I understand how you feel . . ." Then take a moment and argue their case for them. By this I mean tell them why they have a right to feel the way they do.

In arguing their case for them you might say something like this: "I can understand how you feel . . . it isn't inexpensive! And I know that you don't like to spend money when you don't have to because you have to work hard for it."

You could continue by saying, "Many of my other customers felt the same way as you at first—especially when they *only* considered the money involved.

"But when they really examined the *value* and how long the product would last, they found that they were getting a lot for their money."

See how the feel-felt-found formula works?

The first part, the part where you say, "I understand how you feel," is the most important part—especially if you really mean it.

I was in a men's clothing store a few days ago and was looking again at some Oxxford suits. The suits were priced around $1,000 each.

When I commented to the salesperson that the suits certainly cost a lot of money, he responded in a very professional manner. He said, "Yes, they are quite a bit of money!

Obviously you can buy three or four fairly nice suits for what one of these will cost. But the fabric in these suits is far superior to most other suits. All the stitching is hand sewn. And what that means is that they'll outwear other suits several times over. Plus, you'll look and feel much better in one. So . . . when you look at the overall value they really aren't all that expensive."

He didn't argue with me, he agreed with me. He didn't look down his nose at me or try to make me feel cheap. He didn't say it in a condescending tone. He was very nice.

He completely neutralized my objection.

The feel-felt-found formula works because it addresses one of our strongest needs: for others to listen to us without bias and then understand how we feel.

The truth is that we can change other people faster by listening to how they feel and letting them know that we understand them. While it may not be logical, this method works much better than arguing or taking issue with people.

You can't talk people into changing their minds, but you can often listen them into changing.

Now you probably can't always think fast enough to go through all three steps of the feel-felt-found formula, but you can always remember how to do the first step. You can always remember to say, "I understand how you feel . . . ," and then argue their case for them. Tell them why they have a right to feel the way they do.

Another suggestion for handling negative responses or objections is to have people repeat their objections and then to clarify certain points. This gets them talking and you listening. Often they'll talk out their objections, and often after verbalizing objections, they no longer seem so important.

Identify Specific Objections

The next action guide is: Identify specific objections—get the prospect's agreement that these are the only ones.

Objections can best be dealt with when you know exactly what the problem is. Very often the objection you get isn't the real one, it's just one that sounds good.

So in order to identify the real objections, here are a couple of suggestions.

First, ask a question like, "In addition to this problem or objection, are there other issues that we need to think about?"

Or, here's another question, "Is this the only problem or objection that we have to solve?"

Questions like this identify and hopefully isolate the real problems to be solved.

Discuss Possible Solutions

The next action guide is: Discuss possible solutions—ask prospect's opinion of the best solutions.

Often in conflicts, the focus stays on the problem to be solved, rather than the *solution* to be found.

If a person really isn't interested in looking into solutions, that person probably doesn't have sufficient desire or interest.

Think about this for a moment. Often in what we think is the Negotiation step, people keep dragging up excuses or additional objections.

When this begins to happen it often shows a lack of interest on the person's part. So rather than being in the Negotiation step, what you find is that you never really did the Interview step well enough to get them to admit their needs.

So, after you answer an objection and a prospect begins to "fishtail" on you, you can be reasonably sure that that prospect lacks interest or hasn't admitted a strong need.

As long as a person talks in terms of problems rather than solutions, warning signals should go up in your mind.

It's usually only when a person talks in terms of possible solutions that you have a strong prospect.

Focus on Solutions Rather Than on Problems

The question, "What are some possible solutions?" can give you a good indication of your prospect's genuine interest in proceeding.

Often when they respond by talking in terms of possible solutions, they sell themselves. They work through their objections, fears, or hesitancy of buying.

I once worked with a person who had an unusual way of working through problems. It was a very successful way of avoiding arguments or allowing egos to torpedo things.

Whenever problems came up, rather than allowing the focus to stay on them, this person would say "Okay, let's problem-solve! What are some possible solutions?"

Immediately the focus was put on solutions rather than on problems.

Think about what I've just said. You'll see that this is a very important principle of negotiation—keep the focus on solutions rather than on problems.

What you'll learn is that you can *tell* people what the best solutions are all year long, and you may never convince them or change their minds. *But when you ask their opinions* for possible solutions and then for the best solution, you stand a far greater chance of a successful negotiation.

So, always try to steer the conversation away from arguing about problems or objections and instead toward seeking solutions jointly.

There's a powerful principle here: You can usually get a better settlement from people when you ask them for their opinion about the best solution.

Yes, I know that this doesn't always work. Some people are hard and unyielding and won't give an inch. But my belief is that most people will respond because it's a normal instinct to respond in kind.

These ideas can help you increase your negotiating effectiveness and your success in selling. So much of your selling success depends upon how well you negotiate.

Proper Interviewing Reduces Negotiation

Now, let me repeat that often when we think we're in the Negotiation stage, we discover that we really haven't Interviewed properly.

Often when we get stalls and objections we realize that we should have asked more qualifying questions in the Interview step. When you discover this, you might want to stop, go back and ask more Interview questions.

Often we discover that we didn't ask questions like:

> "Who else besides you will be in on the final decision?"
> "What is your approximate budget?"
> "What general price range were you thinking of?"
> "Is the initial price your most important consideration?"
> "What are other factors that you'll consider before making a decision?"

It could be time well spent to analyze the most common objections you get and then get that information during your Interview.

In Conclusion

I've presented a lot of ideas for you to assimilate and apply. You can best retain them as unconscious selling skills by following these ideas:

1. Read this chapter several times during the next week.
2. Write down the action guides on an index card and practice them each day this week—especially the feel-felt-found formula.
3. Get people focusing on solutions rather than on problems.
4. Keep your ego out of the way. Don't get combative or argumentative.

In the next chapter you'll learn about how to negotiate with different styles of buyers. In it you'll learn some important ideas that will help you smooth out objections so you can enjoy an effective close.

INTEGRITY SELLING
SUCCESS PRINCIPLE

People are more apt to negotiate when you ask their opinions than when you press your opinions!

10

How to Negotiate with
Different Styles of Buyers

As you negotiate problems and objections with people,
you'll want to remember these simple guidelines about different buyer styles:

1. *Talkers* need personal support as they work
   through to a decision.
2. *Doers* want to be convinced of results.
3. *Controllers* want facts and documentation.
4. *Plodders* want plenty of information and time to
   make a decision.

First, let's think of some typical objections that you'll receive from different styles of people.

Considerations Talkers Will Have

The Talker might object by saying:

"I'll have to see how others feel about this."
"I'll need to run this by other people."
"I'll have to make sure everyone likes this."
"I'll have to sell this idea to some other people."

Talkers like to buy from people they like. Their biggest problem is deciding which person to buy from—when two or more people, whom they like, are involved as salespeople. This fear is revealed by statements like "Old Charlie is really going to be mad at me if I buy from you!"

Also since Talkers often have to get financial approval from others, either in their companies, or from their spouses, you'll often get objections that reveal that. So you'll hear statements like "okay, well, let me see if I can come up with the money" or "let me talk it over with so and so."

Summed up, Talkers' objections or problems center around these facts:

1. When it comes to money, they often have to get final approval from others.
2. They fear social disapproval in making decisions.
3. They have conflicts when two or more sellers whom they like are competing to sell them.
4. They want to make sure that everyone's happy with their decisions.

Considerations Doers Will Have

Doers' objections are quite different. Typically Doers don't have problems making decisions. Nor are they overly swayed by fear of social disapproval. They're more concerned with the results or the job getting done than with how satisfied other people are.

A strong Doer ruffles feathers and often rushes in where angels fear to tread. They make decisions and jam them down other people's throats.

So, general types of objections that Doers will give you are these:

> "I'm not totally convinced that this'll work."
> "I think I can get a better deal than you're offering me."
> "Who else has made this work?"
> "We've got to have a faster delivery date."

Often, unless Doers are convinced that you speak with highest authority, they'll want to talk to your supervisors before making a decision.

In short, Doers' objections reveal that you haven't sufficiently Validated how your product or service will cause end-result benefits.

Considerations Controllers Will Have

Controllers' objections come when they feel they don't have enough data or proof. Remember, they want facts, figures, and supporting data. You must satisfy their organized, logical minds before they'll make decisions.

You'll hear these types of questions or objections from Controllers:

"I'm not convinced that you can guarantee the quality."

"We prefer not to buy until we see a successful installation that you've done for another firm."

"I'm unclear on your specifications or warranty."

Controllers will object until they're sure your product or service will give them their desired return on investment. Their objections might sound similar to these:

"Before we make a decision, our engineering department will have to give me a final report of their study."

"Before we make a final decision our financial people will have to verify your figures."

Since Controllers are often very analytical, they may throw out objections like this: "I've been through all your data . . . and there are a couple of points I want to get more clarification on."

Think about these types of objections and you'll see that most of them say:

"I'm not convinced of the return-on-investment we get."

"I'm not sure this will fit in with our plans or objectives."

"I don't have as many facts or details as I need."

Considerations Plodders Will Have

Plodders' objections will center on these concerns:

"Don't rush me . . . I don't want to make a hasty decision."

"I don't want to run any big risks."

"I want to take plenty of time and make sure I've gotten the best price and just the right product."

"I want to make sure I understand everything before making a decision."

Common objections from Plodders are these:

"We've never done it like that before."

"We've always used red widgets and now you're trying to sell us *yellow* ones."

"We've done business with your competition for twenty-nine years and I don't see any reason to change now."

Plodders will also give many variations of "I've got to think about it more" or "I'll have to sleep on it . . . I never make a snap decision."

Where both Controllers and Plodders want lots of details, Plodders want details that give information about your product or service features. They want to know how it's made for the sake of knowing how it's made. Controllers want to know how it's made for the sake of knowing how it'll perform. There's a big difference.

Now, with these quick refreshers about the concerns of the four different styles of buyers, let's think about how you can most effectively negotiate win-win solutions with them. How you can work out the problems that keep them from buying.

How to Work Out People's Problems

As you think about successful Negotiation you'll also want to consider how your own style interacts with your prospect's or customer's style.

The style of person *you* are will interact with others differently.

Since I began selling, over thirty years ago, I've had difficulty negotiating with some people. And, for most of those thirty years I didn't know why.

I now know that I'm a Doer. I like to get things done and I don't like to mess with details or waste time. It drives me crazy to deal with anyone who doesn't make a quick decision. I don't like to haggle. I need proof that something works, and once I have what I consider to be sufficient proof, I'm ready to buy.

But not everyone is like me.

I seem naturally to do pretty well when I negotiate with other Doers and Talkers. But for years I didn't do so well negotiating with Plodders and Controllers.

I remember meeting a classic Controller, back when I owned a furniture store.

One Thursday evening a couple in their early forties came in and were looking at a sofa. The woman picked out one she liked a lot. She got very excited about it. She liked the color and the way it felt when she sat on it. She ran her hand over the fabric enthusiastically, luxuriating in the feel of it.

"I love it," she smiled at her husband.

"How much is it?" he shot back, with a total absence of any positive emotions.

She told him the price . . . reluctantly.

"It's too much," he said sternly.

She wilted. Then she looked at him as if to say, "My mother told me that I shouldn't have married a crumb like you!"

Being a coward, I wanted to run and hide rather than get drawn into the fight that I saw coming.

Turning to me, the man said, "We like the sofa, but it's too much money!"

"Well," I answered, "if you pay cash I can give you a 10-percent discount."

"Ten percent," he howled. "Ten percent! You want to give me ten percent? That's insulting!"

I wanted to hit him!

He went on, "I know what kind of mark up you have on these."

"Oh really? How do you know?" I shot back.

"Because I'm the new manager for Dun and Bradstreet. We handle credit reporting for furniture manufacturers. I know that you mark this stuff up 100 percent.

"And . . ." he went on, "if you want to sell me anything you're going to have to get right on your price . . . or I'll go somewhere else and buy it."

I looked at him for a moment and replied, "Then why don't you just do that? Why don't you just go somewhere else and buy it?"

Guess what? He did! He went somewhere else and bought it! At least I assume he did, because he sure didn't buy from me.

At the time I was proud of myself for not allowing him to push me around. But when I honestly faced the facts, I had to admit that I had lost. In fact, probably we both lost. Because if you could have seen the anger on his wife's face as they left, you'd agree that things probably weren't too wonderful around his house for a few days.

Looking back I can see that his action was a Controller's action.

Contrast that award-winning negotiation strategy with one I completed recently with another Controller.

I'd been retained by his boss, a company president, to conduct an annual conference for sales and management people.

In an interview with the president, who was a strong Doer, he told me that he wanted a program that was strongly motivational. He said, "We need you to help us kick these people in their rears and motivate them to get out and make things happen!"

Doesn't that sound like a classic Doer?

I traveled to his city and we talked about the conference for a couple of hours. We both got all excited and fired up.

Then he wanted me to visit with his executive vice president and give him a "good selling!"

Well, it didn't take me two minutes to see that the second-in-control person had totally different ideas of how an annual meeting should be run.

I got the quick feeling that his main objective was to torpedo what the president and I had planned. You didn't have to be too bright or quick to realize there was a problem when his first words were, "We don't want any more of that sales-training or motivational stuff! We want a productive conference, not a circus!"

As I looked around his office I saw all the classic Controller signs. Everything was in neat piles. He could make a 360-degree swing and get to anything he wanted—files, addresses, calculator, personal computer, intercom buttons—everything he'd ever need.

His tone of voice showed no feeling. He minced no words, wasted no motion.

Carefully reflecting back to him the same behavior he modeled, I sat up straight and in a calm, controlled voice said, "I appreciate your being candid and honest with me."

Then I went on, "I'm sure that you're concerned with getting results from our conference—that we not waste time and money and the resources of your people."

"Yeah," he responded.

"I understand," I said. "You want the best return on your investment of money and man hours."

"Yeah," he replied.

Then in a very quiet, yet serious way, I asked him, "As a result of having the conference, what would you like to see happen to your people?"

He began immediately talking about the results he

wanted to happen. I listened, only occasionally asking for clarification.

I asked questions like: "How would you measure the results?" "What are some things we can do in the program to help increase your people's productivity?" "What other specific objectives do you have for the conference?"

He responded to these questions in a very logical way. As he did, it dawned on me that both he and the president were saying the same thing—only in a different language.

By paraphrasing his ideas, in his own style of communicating, I got his agreement on the conference format.

Then when I did the program, both he and the company president were very pleased.

And the reason I was successful with this man was that when I spotted his Controller style, I became a Controller. I talked like one. I thought like one. I became one. I was logical, controlled, no-nonsense, businesslike.

I was able to do this because I'd learned how to spot each style, learned how each style thought and reacted, and learned how to communicate with each style.

And now because I've learned these things I can often become like the person with whom I'm talking. I can often think, talk and view the world as they do.

See the World Through Another Person's Eyes

I've found that when I can see the world through the eyes of another person combativeness and resistance often disappear.

Think for a moment and you'll agree that there's a natural mismatch or resistance between different styles of people. Most people probably won't consciously identify this resistance, but it's there nonetheless—usually at the intuitive level.

Because of this natural resistance, ego clashes occur, combativeness often results, miscommunication results.

It's logical that when you mirror back to others their own style you remove this resistance. As a result, negotiation becomes smoother.

In the last chapter, I presented the feel-felt-found formula. We thought about how you strengthen empathy and smooth out differences by using it.

Now for a moment or two, let's look at an even more in-depth way to use the formula.

Customize Feel-Felt-Found to Your Buyer

Read these sample role-playing situations and see if you can spot the type buyer that each would fit:

> *Objection:* "Well this sounds good . . . but before I can give you the go-ahead, I've got to make sure that all the department heads feel good about it."
>
> *Your response:* "I understand how you feel. It is important to the overall team spirit for your department heads to all be in agreement. Most of my clients in your position of personnel manager have felt the same way until they found that their people appreciated them for making a decision that makes their jobs easier. So . . . why don't you go ahead with your approval?"

Here's another sample:

> *Objection:* "Well . . . this sounds good, but I don't feel I have enough information to make a quick decision. Why don't you get back to me in a couple weeks?"

Your response: "I understand how you feel. You shouldn't make snap decisions. Many of my other customers have felt the same way as you. They didn't want to make rash decisions. And you shouldn't either. But when they found that our unconditional guarantee eliminates the risks of buying, they felt comfortable going ahead and making a decision. What other information can I get for you before you make your decision?"

Here's another:

Objection: "Well . . . all this sounds good, but your price is still a little high!"

Your response: "I understand how you feel. The price isn't inexpensive. This new system will demand a significant investment on your part. Most of the people who have purchased this new system felt the same as you at first until they stopped and considered that this new state-of-the-art model will speed up the productivity and efficiency of your people about three times more than the old one. So . . . you can see while your original investment may be significant, you'll realize very quick payout and return on your investment. So . . . what other concerns do we need to explore before we place your order?"

Here's another:

Objection: "Well . . . this sounds good, but this is a lot more money that you want us to spend, and besides all that, we don't have time to take our people out of production!"

Your response: "I understand how you feel. This will take some time and, frankly, it'll cost quite a few dollars. The president of the Ajax Company felt the same when I first visited with him. But when he tested our program with a sample group of his people and found that their productivity increased 22 percent, he decided that it was a program he wanted his company to have. May I get him on the telephone now and let him share with you his views on the increased profits he's realizing?"

Well . . . if you've carefully read these role-playing situations, you saw clearly the four different styles of buyers—how each looks through different sets of eyes. And how to deal with each style in the appropriate way.

In Conclusion

So, to sum up this chapter, let me list these important points:

1. Know the general types of considerations and objections different styles will have.
2. Step into each person's world. See it from their perspective. Think their style, talk their style, become their style.
3. Fit your feel-felt-found to each buyer's individual style.

As you learn, observe and master these skills in this chapter your success will increase. Your effectiveness and confidence will also grow to higher levels.

Read this chapter several times this week. Role-play how you could have applied the ideas to people you've tried to sell. Doing this will program your subconscious to react instinctively later.

Keep doing this and gradually you'll increase your skills in negotiating with different styles of buyers.

INTEGRITY SELLING
SUCCESS PRINCIPLE

People are more apt to see your side of the argument when you first see their side!

11

How to Close Sales

Closing is the most difficult action that many salespeople have to perform. It should be the *easiest!*

So . . . what's the problem?

As I've said before, it seems to me that most salespeople have been programmed to view selling as a strategy where they do something *to* someone. With this slant on selling the close becomes the main focus.

You'll find books in most bookstores that present selling as a series of strategies to help salespeople do a number on people. It pits salespeople against buyers. The focus is on tricky, gimmicky maneuvers to outsmart people and get them to buy.

The sales process is often presented as an adversarial relationship, rather than a trust relationship. It's presented where the salesperson scores at someone's expense.

Again the whole focus is doing something *to* someone that causes them to buy.

Then add the cliches like "Close Early and Often!" that you'll find in certain books, and you set in motion tons of confusion in salespeople. How about this gem: "The sale begins when the customer says no."

Tricky Closing Tactics Don't Work

Not only do these manipulative concepts not work for most of us, but they cause a great deal of damage to sales-people.

They create a cognitive dissonance in salespeople—conflicts that torpedo their success.

Manipulative selling runs against the grain of most people's value systems. The only people's values that aren't disturbed by tricky selling tactics are people who lack integrity. Said another way, when we train salespeople to do Integrity Selling, their self-esteem rises; immediately they feel better about themselves.

Call-reluctance and fear of rejection in closing are the biggest roadblocks to the success of most salespeople. And call-reluctance rises as salespeople view the sales process as manipulative.

When you understand this important concept, you'll clearly understand more of the power of Integrity Selling.

Value-Focus Reduces Call-Reluctance

When our focus is to create value for people, our call-reluctance and fear of rejection are reduced.

More specifically, when we approach people, identify their needs, demonstrate, validate and work out problems by win-win negotiation—and we totally believe that purchasing from us will create value for them—we'll have little fear of asking for a closing decision.

Our reluctance diminishes. Think about that for a moment. This can powerfully influence our selling success.

Let's use these ideas as a springboard into this lesson on closing.

What Integrity Closing Is

Let me tell you my definition of integrity closing: Closing is simply asking for a decision when you're pretty sure a person is going to say, "Yes."

Let me repeat this. *Closing is simply asking for a decision when you're pretty sure a person is going to say, "Yes."*

Think about that for a moment.

In the AID, Inc. system of selling, you should never ask for a decision until you've completed all the first five steps. Until you've Approached, Interviewed, Demonstrated, Validated, and Negotiated, you should never try to Close. Also, never ask for a decision until you're pretty sure you'll get a "yes."

Think for a moment about times when people bought from you . . . I'll bet most of the time before they said, "yes," *you already knew that they would.*

The reason you knew was that they'd given you plenty of feedback and positive signals—either in words or in body language.

In a moment we'll talk about ways you can know the right time to ask for a decision.

Closing Action Guides

But first, let's think of the action guides for the Closing step. They are:

1. Ask trial-closing questions that get opinions and response.
2. Give positive reinforcement.
3. Restate how benefits will outweigh costs.
4. Ask for a decision.

Trial-closing questions are very different from closing questions.

In what way?

Trial-Closing Questions Call for Opinions

Trial-closing questions call for *opinions.* Closing questions call for *decisions.*

One calls for opinions. The other calls for decisions. There's a big difference.

You can begin asking trial-closing questions in your Demonstration step. As you demonstrate your product or service you can ask questions like:

"How does this look to you?"
"How do you like this feature?"
"Is this what you had in mind?"
"How important is this to you?"

These and other similar trial-closing questions simply ask for response—for opinions.

You can also ask opinion-getting questions in the Validation and Negotiation steps.

Not only will this give you lots of information that you need to have, but you'll also develop stronger trust. A deeper trust bond is developed as you ask questions and listen to people.

When customers talk and you listen, it creates the best sales environment you can structure.

So consciously ask opinion questions from your demonstration to just before closing.

Reinforce All Positive Responses You Get

And as you ask trial-close questions and get opinions and response, learn to give positive reinforcement.

How do you give positive reinforcement? Several ways. You give positive reinforcement anytime you acknowledge what people tell you—anytime you let them know that you listened and that you heard.

You can acknowledge or give feedback to people by nodding approval. By verbalizing agreement. By paraphrasing what people tell you. By using gestures that show you heard what they said.

Why should you perform these actions?

First, this causes you to really listen to what people tell you.

Second, it proves to them that you listened to and remembered what they said.

Third, it influences even deeper levels of customer persuasion. It heightens rapport and trust. It lowers natural resistance.

Listening Fills Needs People Have

One of the greatest psychological needs people have is for other people to listen to them without bias—to totally listen. Not just listen waiting for a chance to argue a point or jump in and resume our talking, but totally listen without bias or assumptions. This is one of your customer's greatest needs.

The truth is that when we fill this need for people, they'll unconsciously want to fill our needs. And the best way for them to do that is to listen to *us* without bias.

So my point again is: *Asking opinion questions and totally listening is a powerful method of persuasion.*

When you do this kind of total, in-depth listening you're going to know where your customers or prospects are. They're going to give you plenty of clues.

When you've had positive clues as to what a person's decision will be, then and only then is it time to ask for a decision.

But, let's be honest . . . you're going to have times when you think they'll say yes, but they don't. Usually when this happens, you'll find that you haven't completed a prior step. Your customer's stalls or objections may give you these insights:

- You don't perceive their needs as they do . . . or you didn't Interview well.
- You didn't Demonstrate what they perceive will fill their needs.
- You didn't Validate to where they were convinced.
- You didn't Negotiate an acceptable solution.

Not long ago I worked with a major company in designing a training program. Several months had gone by, lots of work had been done, several meetings took place, terms were negotiated, and contracts drawn. Everything had been approved and was ready to sign.

After all this time had elapsed, after I thought all the bases had been covered, out of the clear blue sky the chief decision-maker looked at me one day and said, "But this isn't what I want!"

I was stunned, as were all the other people.

All of a sudden it dawned on me that I hadn't completely done the Interview step several weeks earlier.

A Negative Response at Closing Reveals Your Interview Wasn't Completed

Think for a moment about responses we get just when it's time to Close.

Responses like "I've got to look around" show that you didn't Interview, Demonstrate, or Validate well.

"I've got to get approval from others" shows that you didn't find out who the decision-makers were in your Interview.

A principle here is *never ask for a decision unless you're in front of people who can make a buying decision.*

Responses like "it's too much money" tell you you didn't negotiate well or that they didn't see value in your offering.

If you get sudden objections when you attempt to close, it shows you that you didn't complete a prior step.

So instead of combatively trying to change someone's mind, you should identify the step you missed and go back and attempt to complete it.

Restate How the Benefits Will Outweigh the Costs

Assuming that it's time to ask for a decision, the third action guide is: Restate how the benefits will outweigh the costs.

It's important to remember that before people buy anything, or agree to anything, they must first weigh the benefits against the cost.

When I use the word "cost" I mean more than just money. I include with money things like time, risk involved, and hassle. All these go together to make up the cost.

So remember that people will always weigh the benefits against the cost.

Think of it as a balance scale where on one side we put the cost and on the other side we put the benefits or value.

Make sure *before* you ask for a decision that the person is picturing the value outweighing the cost.

Doing this will strongly impact your closing for two main reasons.

First, it will cause you to be more aware of benefits instead of features. And second, it will help you be more aware of all the elements included in the cost to your customer.

It will help you see things from your customer's view that will in turn help your customers see things from your view.

Ask for a Decision . . . at the Right Time

When you receive positive feedback from your customer and you think it's time to close, you can do so by simply asking for a decision.

Remember, our definition of closing is simply asking for a decision at the right time.

You can feel very good about asking . . . if what you want them to do will give value to them.

In fact, if what you're offering them will create value for them, you have a professional responsibility to ask them. You owe that to them!

When you ask, here are three ways to ask with integrity. They are:

1. The assumptive Close
2. The either-or Close
3. The simply-ask Close.

The Assumptive Close

The assumptive Close asks for a minor decision, assuming that they've already made a positive major buying decision.

Here's a typical assumptive Close:

> "In addition to the things we've discussed, is there anything we need to consider before we finalize this transaction?" (You insert your needed closing action—check, purchase order, signing contract, etc.)

Another type of assumptive Close might go like this:

> "When will you want us to deliver this?"

Another might be:

> "When would you like to have this installed and fully functioning?"

You can think of many other assumptive Closes. It would be time well spent to sit down and design three to six specific assumptive Closes that you can memorize and use in your selling.

It's a very powerful, yet subtle way to ask for a decision when asked out of an integrity base.

The Either-Or Close

The either-or Close asks someone to make a choice between two items or products.

Here's a couple of sample either-or questions:

"Do you want this television set with the remote control . . . or without it?"

"Do you want me to include the family-income rider in your policy . . . or not?"

So you see, this Close asks them to make a choice between two items, two products, or two things.

The Simply-Ask Close

The third close is the simply-ask Close. In it you simply ask for the appropriate closing action.

When people buy from you, what action do they take? Do they give you a check, sign a contract, give you a purchase order, or give you a verbal commitment?

The simply-ask Close gets you simply asking them to take the appropriate closing action.

You might ask:

"May we then get the contract signed so I can go ahead and order your unit?"

"May I have your check for a down payment?"

"How do I get a purchase order?"

You simply ask for the appropriate closing action.

Again . . . closing is simply asking for a decision at the right time.

And when I say "the right time," I mean the right time for your customer.

In Integrity Selling, our motivation to close isn't just to make a sale or score. If our focus is truly on creating value for a customer, then our close has to be consistent.

Consistency, or congruence, means that we only ask for a decision when value will be created for our prospects.

Again, we need to consider the style of buyer as we close.

Here are a few suggestions about closing the four styles of buyers.

How to Close Talkers

First, Talkers will not make a decision totally based on facts and information. Their decision to buy will be based more on feelings than logic. They'll hate to turn you down or reject you. Often they won't come right out with a "no," but will stall around.

Talkers prefer to buy from people whom they trust and feel good about. They're influenced more by the people they buy from than by other styles.

Before you can expect a decision from them, you often have to have other people who support them in on the decision. Many Talkers want help in making decisions.

And . . . be sure and remember their need for social acceptance when you ask them to buy.

How to Close Doers

Doers are usually ready to make a quick decision once they think they have the information they need. If you've done the Validation and Negotiation steps well, you can ask Doers to buy quickly and directly.

"Let's wrap this up." "All I need is your signature." "If you'll okay this, I'll attend to all the details."

Ask Doers to take the appropriate closing action—the simply-ask Close. The assumptive Close fits Doers as well.

Remember . . . when you're selling Doers, be sure and take as many details as possible off their shoulders.

Before you ask for a buying decision, be sure they're satisfied with the information. They'll make decisions from their gut feeling, but they have to feel they have a grasp of all facts and information.

They like for you to be direct with them. So don't stall around, or be wishy-washy or indirect.

Closing pressure can often backfire with Doers. If they feel pressured they may tell you to go jump in the lake.

How to Close Controllers

Before you ask Controllers for a decision, first make sure they have all the facts they demand. Make sure you've discussed the risks involved. Don't try to *minimize* the risks, just show them that the risks are less than the benefits. Always ask Controllers, "Is there any other information I can get for you before you make a decision?"

Controllers don't like to be pushed. Closing pressure will also backfire with them. Too much pressure applied will cause them to cut you off coolly and send you on your way.

But Controllers will usually make fast decisions once they feel they have all the facts. They won't be swayed by emotions. Emotions don't enter into their decisions.

When you ask them for a decision, be direct. If they're not ready to make a decision ask them when they will be. They'll usually honor time frames they commit to.

How to Close Plodders

When you're working with Plodders, remember that they don't like change. They resist change. Neither are they risk takers. So don't expect them to buy things that are going to cause change or high risk.

Also, you can expect Plodders to be slow in making buying decisions. They'll want to "sleep on it," or take time to think things through.

In working with Chevrolet salespeople, we helped many of them increase their closes dramatically by identifying buyer styles and closing consistently with the styles they identify.

For instance, we found many salespeople missing closes with Plodders because they put too much pressure on them. When they didn't decide quickly, which they never do, the salespeople wrote them off.

But when they realized that Plodders need time, and when they gave them time and followed up on them, their closings of Plodders increased significantly.

Give Plodders time. Don't pressure them. They'll react negatively to selling pressure. But stay with them and follow up with patience.

While we're on the subject of selling pressure, let me make a couple of observations.

First, the level of trust and rapport you have with your customer will influence their perception of selling pressure. If you have high trust and rapport, selling pressure will be perceived as low. But if trust and rapport is weak, any selling pressure will be perceived as high or undesirable.

So . . . again, we see the importance of trust and rapport in Integrity Selling.

In Conclusion

Let me conclude this message by repeating that closing is simply asking for a decision at the right time.

And then, let me encourage you to:

1. Read this chapter several times this week.
2. Write down the action guides on a card.
3. Think about the concepts of closing that I've mentioned.
4. Apply these concepts in your selling this week.

As you adopt these Integrity Selling concepts of closing your self-esteem will rise, your call-reluctance will decrease, your trust and rapport will be strong and your pressure perceived as low.

And . . . your sales closures will take some dramatic leaps upward.

INTEGRITY SELLING
SUCCESS PRINCIPLE

People are more apt to say "yes" when trust and rapport are high than when selling pressure is high!

12

How to Maximize Your Earnings
with This Book

In this chapter, I want to mention several ideas that can help you increase your own personal prosperity.

Since so much of selling is psychological, these ideas will help you keep your own personal belief system healthy and positive. These ideas work on the causal level, not on the effect level. They'll contribute to your success.

Here are three ways you can maximize your earnings:

1. Sell a product or service that you're sold on.
2. Associate with people who are now earning what you want to earn.
3. Set sales and motivational goals.

As I've observed successful salespeople, I've seen some common ingredients. For one, most of them are selling a product or service that excites them. They almost become missionaries. They believe in the integrity of whatever they're selling. They want people to have it and enjoy it.

On the other hand, salespeople who jump from one product to another, with little loyalty or commitment, don't do so well.

I've seen many salespeople sell things just to be selling things. There was no loyalty, commitment, or pride in what they sold. It was just a job.

And I've seen salespeople sell products or services because they were low priced. There was no particular pleasure or emotional satisfaction, they just sold them as commodities.

But my overwhelming belief is that big league salespeople —the ones who make high incomes—are successful because of a desire to deliver value to people. And because they believe their product or service will do it!

Recently I was in a car dealership interviewing the owner. The dealer was a Controller style. He was also cynical and negative. He griped about everything.

At one point he referred to the cars he sold as "junk," adding to that the statement: "I wouldn't drive one of these if I wasn't selling 'em!"

That certainly impressed me!

My unasked question was, "Then why don't you sell another kind that you *do* like?"

Recently I conducted some sales training sessions for a firm. One of their salespeople had worked for a competitive firm and lost no opportunity to knock them.

A few months later I went back in and found that he had quit and gone back to the competitor that he had given such negative reviews to before.

My question to you is this: If you went into either of these people's businesses, do you think they'd reveal their lack of conviction of their products' integrity? Do you think you might get some silent messages that might fall short in impressing you?

Associate with Successful People

The second point I mentioned was: To maximize your earnings, *associate with people who are now earning what you want to earn.*

This is one of the most powerful success principles I know.

Let's think about it for a few moments. In fact, let me introduce a very profound truth to you. It's this: All sales-people sell in a manner consistent with their belief systems!

You see . . . we each have a well-formed, although unconscious, belief about ourselves and our possibilities.

Dr. Maxwell Maltz, the author of the bestseller, *Psycho-Cybernetics,* said it like this: "We each have a distinct self-image. It's the sort of person we conceive ourselves to be. And our self-image controls all our actions, feelings, behavior and ability."

For seven years, from 1968 until 1975, when he passed away, I had the privilege of working closely with Dr. Maltz. A deeper understanding of this principle was one of the great gifts he gave me. This concept has had a dramatic impact on my training.

Our Personal Belief System Influences Our Sales

This well-defined, although unconscious, belief system controls all our actions, feelings, behavior and abilities. Through it, we see ourselves performing in well-defined levels.

"I should sell so much!" "I'm capable of earning so much!" "I relate best to these kind of people!" These and many other unconscious assumptions, or beliefs, control all our actions, feelings, behavior, and abilities!

I'll never forget an incident that happened several years ago to a friend. He was in the life insurance business and had survived but had never really sold up to his potential.

A very honest, decent person, he became associated with a successful businessman through a church project. Not long after that the businessman called him one day and told him that his tax attorney had told him that he needed to purchase a million dollar life insurance policy.

He asked my friend if he would come by and write it.

This was back several years ago, when a million dollar policy was not exactly a daily sales activity.

My friend wrote it. This qualified him to attend the Million Dollar Round Table annual convention and rub shoulders with the top people in his industry.

Because of this experience he began to relate to top performers. His level of self-belief changed. His mental image expanded.

And the interesting thing is that for the next ten years in a row he made the Million Dollar Round Table.

His new belief system caused him to sell at new levels.

Our sales performance is usually consistent with our own personal belief system. Expand our belief systems and we *automatically* expand our sales and income.

Everything Seems Impossible
Until You See a Success!

Ralph Waldo Emerson wrote this most significant truth, "Everything seems impossible until you see a success!"

It's also true that when we associate with others who earn what we want to earn, it makes it seem more possible for us. When we see their successes, our success seems more possible.

I've given this advice out at seminars only to have an occasional person ask, "Yeah well, that sounds good, but why would a person who's more successful than we are want to spend time with us?"

That's a good question.

Personally I've found that successful people are usually glad to share their knowledge with others who want to learn from them. Notice I said *who want to learn from them.* I've had several very successful people become customers or close friends because I asked them to share their wisdom, knowledge, and experience with me—and because I listened.

Another tip is to get together weekly with two or three other people who have similar goals and achievement drives as you have. Have breakfast or lunch.

In these support meetings share your successes and learning experiences. Become avid readers of self-help books. Listen to self-help tapes. Talk about what you're learning, but more importantly, how you're applying what you're learning.

After sharing your learning experiences, build up and reinforce each other. Mention strengths and growth areas you're seeing in each other.

Keep your meetings on the subject of personal growth and learning. Keep all conversation on positive themes. Don't let negative talk enter into your conversations—it will kill the effectiveness of your meetings.

Try these ideas. Perform them to the letter. When you do you'll notice an almost immediate increase in your own self-esteem. Your self-image will expand. And when these things happen, your prosperity will grow.

Set Sales and Motivational Goals

The third way you can maximize your earnings and create greater prosperity in your career is to *set sales and motivational goals.*

Everyone knows the power of setting specific sales and income goals. You've been taught this in sales meetings, seminars, and self-help books. As a result you probably set weekly, monthly, quarterly, and annual goals.

And, you should! But while these goals generate motivation and help release achievement drive, there's another technique that will help, as well.

Learn to set motivational goals!

Motivational goals are rewards you'll give yourself when you reach your sales goals. It's very important for us to set such goals and then carry through and reward ourselves when they are reached.

I was really hit with the power of this concept several years ago when I had the chance to work with and learn from a very wealthy man, W. Clement Stone.

He talked about this concept several times before the full impact of his message hit me.

One day I was visiting with Mike Ritt. Mike had been with Mr. Stone's life insurance company for more than thirty years. He'd worked closely with Napoleon Hill, author of the self-help classic *Think and Grow Rich,* when Hill and Mr. Stone worked together.

Mike kept the archives of all of Hill's tapes and filmed presentations.

I asked Mike how Mr. Stone had become so successful at motivating salespeople.

He thought for a moment and then told me this story:

"First of all, Mr. Stone learned the art of motivation for himself. In his early days of personal selling he'd obligate himself or purchase something that would cause him to have to go out and work hard in order to pay for it.

"And then later in his career, when he was working directly with salespeople and sales managers, he'd take them out and get them to buy things they wanted—new cars or stock in his company. Then he'd teach them how to use that obligation as self-motivation that would cause them to work hard and produce."

Mike went on, "He believed that an honest man would pay his debts, and when an honest man is in debt he'll work hard to get out."

I've thought of this example many times, and it seems to me that this concept of motivating ourselves by rewards is a bit of positive self-reinforcement that can contribute to the success of any salesperson.

I've tried it many times. I've promised myself short-term rewards like a new briefcase, a gold pen, or a trip for my wife and myself. I've promised myself new cars for reaching major sales goals, as well as clothes, or time off.

And when I've reached the sales goals I've been very careful to pay myself.

I must admit that often, after reaching the goal, the reward that motivated me didn't seem as important as it had before. And there's often a temptation to forgo the reward and start immediately working toward a higher goal. But regardless of the temptation, it's important to follow through and give yourself the reward.

This positive self-reinforcement is critical for building continual self-motivation.

How Can You Set Motivational Goals?

Well, how about you? How can you set sales and motivation goals? How can you reward yourself for reaching short-term—and longer-term—goals? What can you promise yourself for exceeding your sales goals this next month?

What might you give yourself when you reach your annual sales goals? And what might you give yourself if you make a large sale that's the result of extra effort?

Answering these questions, and then taking action and

carrying through on them, can have a dramatic impact on your selling success.

And as we think about goal-setting . . . let me say this: With Value-Focused selling, part of our goals should be how much and what kind of value we can give to our clients, customers, or prospects.

This could begin with a mission or purpose statement stating the kind and quality of value you give your customers. Then it might get more specific and become an important part of your goals.

In Conclusion

In this chapter I've said that you can have a positive impact on your sales success by practicing three suggestions. They are:

1. Sell a product or service that you're sold on.
2. Associate with people who are now earning what you want to earn.
3. Set sales and motivational goals.

I gave you some quick ideas about how to apply these suggestions.

But ideas can't be converted into income until they're acted upon!

I suggest that you reread this chapter and carefully consider the three suggestions I made. Then, take action on one or all that are appropriate for you.

The reflection and self-examination will be good for you. Your sales career will be better as a result. And, you'll find that these actions will strongly influence your success in selling.

Afterword

Almost each week I do sales-training seminars for organizations. Several hundred independent consultants market and conduct training programs that I have written. Through these I get lots of feedback from salespeople.

Many of them are looking for magic tricks, gimmicks, or manipulative strategies that will be an "open sesame" to their sales and earnings success. They're looking for external techniques that will give them an ace up on competition.

And they miss the most basic cause of selling success!

In my opinion, the cause of success in selling is the *integrity* level of the salesperson. I can't sell above who I am—I can only sell consistent with the quality of person I am.

In this regard, one of my favorite quotations is from Ralph Waldo Emerson's essay "Self-Reliance." In it he wrote:

> We pass for what we are. Character teaches above
> our wills. Men imagine that they communicate

their virtue or vice only by overt actions, and do
not see that virtue or vice emit a breath every moment.

We pass for *what* we are. We succeed consistent with
who we are. Causes and effects always seem to balance
themselves. And integrity is the main contributor to selling
success!

Everything in this book has been intended to contribute
to your Integrity Selling—from the basic philosophy to the
strategies and action guides.

In the beginning, I said that the question of sales success
has more to do with values and ethics than strategies and
techniques. I mentioned that we're seeing massive cultural
and value shifts in the world today. And that these shifts
are demanding a new kind of selling—Integrity Selling.

I gave you the AID, Inc. system of selling that actually
becomes a value-based road map to Integrity Selling.

I mentioned ten points of Integrity Selling values and ethics. A few of the major points were:

1. Selling is an exchange of value.
2. Understanding people's wants or needs always
   precedes any attempt to sell.
3. Selling techniques give way to selling principles.

Some results of our research were sprinkled throughout
the book. One important point was, where trust and rapport
are high, there's almost never any perceived selling pressure! And, where trust and rapport are low, any selling
pressure is perceived as being high!

You learned about Value-Focused selling: how we all
have an unconscious central sales focus that eventually influences our success level. You learned that your success is
enhanced by having a value-focus.

I shared with you the four styles of buyers—Talkers, Doers, Controllers, Plodders. You learned that each thinks differently, acts differently and makes decisions differently.

You learned that your own style can either match or mismatch your prospect's style. And you learned that success comes when you identify and match the style of the person you're selling.

Will This Book Contribute to Your Sales Success?

Within the messages of this book, I've given you enough techniques and information to dramatically increase your sales success—regardless of your current level of success.

But I must be very honest with you! I must tell you that many of the salespeople who read this book probably won't enjoy any real changes in their sales performance.

They won't . . . because of one simple fact! They won't take the time to *assimilate* and *apply* the ideas into their selling behavior.

Think about that for a moment!

I talk to lots of people who can quote sales books, tapes, or speakers. They seem to know a great deal about selling. But I only have to ask a couple questions to find out that while they may know a lot about selling, they don't *sell* a lot!

And the reason is that they've never bridged from *knowing* to *doing*—from *knowledge* to *practice.*

Knowledge Isn't Valuable
Until It's Channeled into Habits

This is why I've asked you to read each chapter of this book several times for a week—to apply the ideas in your selling. Then analyze, inspect and learn from your practice.

As you concentrate your efforts, and as you read and

practice, you'll begin to build positive habits. The repetition of reading and practicing is critical for automatic sales habits to be formed. So is the concentration of your efforts on one chapter for one week.

If you understand what I've just said, and if you do it as I've outlined, you'll be repaid for the price of this book many thousand times over in the years to come.

And I'll have reached my goal of creating high value for you—of giving you much more than you've paid for this book.

So . . . good luck to you. Keep reading and practicing. Recognize, relate, assimilate, and apply. Don't be content with just learning. Demand of yourself that you make these concepts a part of your automatic sales habits.

As you do these suggestions, your success, your sales, your self-esteem, and your prosperity will all skyrocket!

And Finally

Emerson also wrote, "No man can learn what he has not preparation for learning."

I've learned that we hear what we're prepared to hear. We learn what we're prepared to learn. We discover and comprehend what we're prepared to discover and comprehend.

My hope is that either you were prepared for this book . . . or you'll keep reading it until you become prepared.

In either case, my hope is that you'll soon enjoy expanded prosperity in your life.

I'd welcome your comments or questions:

Ron Willingham
Ron Willingham Courses, Inc.
4705 N. 65th Street
Scottsdale, Arizona 85253